T0129172

MIGHTY

MATT CROFTON

MIGHTY
ONE MAN'S QUEST TO CONQUER THE MISSISSIPPI RIVER

iUniverse books may be ordered through booksellers or by contacting:

iUniverse
1663 Liberty Drive
Bloomington, IN 47403
www.iuniverse.com
1-800-Authors (1-800-288-4677)

Because of the dynamic nature of the Internet, any web addresses or links contained in this book may have changed since publication and may no longer be valid. The views expressed in this work are solely those of the author and do not necessarily reflect the views of the publisher, and the publisher hereby disclaims any responsibility for them.

Any people depicted in stock imagery provided by Thinkstock are models, and such images are being used for illustrative purposes only.
Certain stock imagery © Thinkstock.

ISBN: 978-1-5320-2982-0 (sc)
ISBN: 978-1-5320-2981-3 (e)

Library of Congress Control Number: 2017914780

Print information available on the last page.

iUniverse rev. date: 12/06/2017

For Aden and Ella
My Life's Greatest Adventure

"Twenty years from now you will be more disappointed by the things that you didn't do than by the ones you did do. So throw off the bowlines. Sail away from the safe harbor. Catch the trade winds in your sails. Explore. Dream. Discover."

MARK TWAIN

Histoplasmosis

HISTOPLASMOSIS is an infection caused by a fungus called Histoplasma. The fungus lives in the environment, particularly in soil that contains large amounts of bird or bat droppings. In the United States, Histoplasma mainly lives in the central and eastern states, especially areas around the Ohio and Mississippi River valleys. The fungus also lives in parts of Central and South America, Africa, Asia, and Australia.

People can get histoplasmosis after breathing in the microscopic fungal spores from the air. Although most people who breathe in the spores don't get sick, those who do may have a fever, cough, and fatigue. Many people who get histoplasmosis will get better on their own without medication, but in people, such as those who have weakened immune systems, the infection can become severe.

Sarcoidosis

SARCOIDOSIS, also called sarcoid, is a auto-immune disease involving abnormal collections of inflammatory cells (granulomas) that can form as nodules in multiple organs. The granulomas are most often located in the lungs or its associated lymph nodes, but any organ can be affected.

The word "sarcoidosis" comes from Greek sarc meaning "flesh", the suffix eidos meaning "type", and sis, a common suffix in Greek meaning "condition". Thus the whole word means "a condition that resembles crude flesh".

These two diseases combined would be called, "The Perfect Storm". Or, in Matt's case, it would become a violent brush with death.

Prologue

Operator: Thank you for calling Frontier Airlines, this is Rosanna, how may I help you?

Me: Hi, Rosanna, I'm trying to book a flight from Orlando to Minneapolis, but I have some unusual cargo.

Operator: What do you want to transport?

Me: It's a stand-up paddleboard. It's like a big surfboard.

Operator: What are the dimensions?

Me: It's twelve feet in length and weighs about thirty-five pounds.

Operator: What is it used for?

Me: To paddle the length of the Mississippi River.

Operator: Excuse me?

Me: To paddle the length of the Mississippi River.

1

Humble Beginnings

In the summer of 2010, I was given less than forty-eight hours to live.

It was a bit on the tragic side... almost fictional. I suffered multiple organ failure and bled out of every hole in my face. The doctors shoved what they described as "nostril tampons" up my nose to stop the blood from emptying out of my head. The blood transfusions could barely keep up with the amount that I was losing. My parents stood by my bed in the ICU as the lead physician informed them that their son would likely die before sunrise.

What a difference a year can make.

Twelve months from the day I was emancipated from life support, I now prepared to enter the fourth largest river in the world on a 35lb plank made of epoxy and foam. My dad was with me, helping to unload my gear from the rental van. I'd never heard of Lake Itasca, but without this small glacial lake, I would never gain access to the source of the Mighty Mississippi.

Lake Itasca. My ambassador to new beginnings.

"Did you know a raindrop that falls in Lake Itasca will arrive at the Gulf of Mexico ninety days later?"

I've already heard this fun-fact three times this morning. I was inside the Itasca State Park Visitor's Center buying some bottled water and overheard a mom reading it to her daughter.

Next, there was a couple walking up the trail from the headwaters talking about the same thing—raindrops and the Mississippi.

Now, I'm hearing it for the third time in relation to my answers given after a friendly passerby succumbed to curiosity and approached me. He asked something along the lines of, "What are you doing with that big surfboard?" I told him and then he laid the raindrop theory on me.

"If a raindrop takes three months, how long would it take a paddleboard?" I asked.

"Can't help you there, brother." He smiled and walked away.

My dad shouldered my packs, I palmed my stand up paddleboard (SUP), and we began hauling fifty-five pounds of gear down the rustic path towards the source of the Mississippi. I was grateful that he decided to follow me to Minnesota and see me off. The original plan was to fly from Orlando to Minneapolis and hitchhike to the headwaters. This was better by far.

As we entered the trailhead, I noticed the first in a series of small wooden signs jutting up from the ground about knee high.

Headwaters 800 Ft.

People passed by us, giving double and triple takes. Some of them asked about the paddleboard. I was happy to tell the story because it was an excuse to drop the gear and catch my breath.

"Where are you going to sleep?" "I've got a one-man tent." I smiled.

"What are you going to eat?"

"Ramen Noodles are light and cheap!" I said.
My dad shouldered my backpack; I hoisted the paddleboard
and we moved on.

Headwaters 600 Ft.

We came to a small bridge and I glanced down at the narrow
creek flowing beneath me. I gestured with my chin towards the
gentle stream.
"That's it?"
My dad grinned, "Humble beginnings, Son."

Headwaters 400 Ft.

We rounded a final bend in the trail and moved into a
clearing where the famous headwater marker came into view.
People flanked the sign, taking photos next to the spot where the
fourth largest river in the world begins its life with about two feet
of water. The marker was in the shape of a tree trunk, painted
brown with mustard yellow letters carved into the face that read:

"Here, 1,475 feet above the ocean, The Mighty Mississippi begins to flow
on its winding way 2,552 miles to the Gulf of Mexico."

Standing at the source on the north end of Lake Itasca, it was
difficult to believe that this meandering trickle (no more than
twenty feet wide), would turn into the Mighty Mississippi; slicing
America in half, before giving herself to the sea.
I tilted Old Blue up on his stern and waited my turn for
pictures so I could commemorate the memory, and get on with
my adventure. I was sore from the walk. I arched my back for a
long stretch and my eyes focused on the sunless morning sky. My
expression more than likely conveyed a sense of discomfort with
the weather. I'd rather not begin a journey in gloom. For some

reason, a sunny, blue sky makes the transition from everyday life into a grand adventure less intimidating. Do clouds float closer to Earth up north? The silver cumulous clouds swirling above me appeared to hover slightly above the tips of the evergreen pines that surrounded Lake Itasca.

I knew the water was going to be cold. I hate cold water. And there was a chance of rain later. Gray skies and cold water—my morale was dwindling, but there was no scrubbing the launch today. Not for weather. Besides, beginning my adventure with a lifeless sky would only help me to appreciate the sun when it finally arrives, cutting through the gray canopy with its golden beams of warmth.

Sun or no sun, I would not allow Mother Nature to have dominion over my mood today. I was about to embark on an extraordinary adventure. I was going to attempt something that nobody had ever done before. On a planet, home to seven billion people, I would be the first person in history to take a SUP down the entire length of the Mississippi River.

A large tree trunk, sliced in half, stretched across the river, posing as a bridge, and I used it to cross to the other side where I found a clearing on the rocky shore. It would be a good place for me to wade into the water and secure my gear to the SUP.

By the time my legs acclimated to the frigid headwaters, a crowd had formed around the crazy man strapping a sleeping bag to a massive surfboard. My dad did most of the talking. I could hear him telling my story as I packed Old Blue.

A little boy with a Minnesotan accent asked if he could stand on my board and take a picture with me. I reach out my hand and helped him from shore, then flashed a peace sign towards his mother who snapped the photo.

The SUP was packed and ready to float. With nothing else to delay my launch, I took a moment to breathe. Time slowed as I scanned the banks of the river. I wanted to absorb the magnanimity of it all: people shooting photos, the look of pride in my father's eyes and the smile on his face, and the peacefulness of a moment without depression. I felt so happy... so free.

I had traveled a long way to get here. I went through several airlines before I could find one that was affordable and could transport my Old Blue. They routed me to Denver and then on to Minneapolis, followed by a four-hour car ride. I started with $1,200 before airfare. Now I was down to eight hundred dollars and still had over twenty-four hundred river miles to go.

Twenty-four hundred miles on eight hundred dollars.

However, the significance of this moment—the culmination of experiences that led to this day, standing kneedeep in the Mississippi River—was more than the physical miles traveled between Orlando and the headwaters. I'm talking about the minutes, hours, days, and years before the conception of this adventure—the trickling of time from childhood into the days of adulthood. And it hasn't been a happy trail.

The truth about me? My life has been a series of failures and lingering sadness from the moment I left high school. The trail of tears eventually led to me nearly dying in a hospital in Utah at the relatively young age of thirty-six. I've never had the satisfaction, that coveted peace within my soul, that everything I've endured was for a reason. Somewhere along the way, I gave bitterness power over happiness. I allowed myself to sink into the lies that life hated me, God hated me and that I would never find true purpose in my life.

But there was always hope.

I stood in the crystal cool waters of the Mississippi and let the butterflies flutter wildly inside my stomach. Adrenaline forged a sharp focus and I suddenly became fully aware of what I was about to do. People began to fade. My father began to fade.

Everything but water began to fade, and I realized, probably for the first time in my life, that I was exactly where I was supposed to be.

"You didn't forget to make a wish, did you?"

I didn't turn around at first. I was still in my focused meditation, making minor adjustments to my gear. My dad was by the bridge talking to a man who worked for National Geographic. That's when a woman asked the question and there was no way I could have fathomed its significance at the time.

"A wish?" I replied while fogging my sunglasses before wiping them against my shirt.

"Of course! When you walk across the headwaters, you make a wish, and your wish will come true by the time the waters that wet your legs reach the Gulf of Mexico."

I looked up just as the slender, blonde thirty-something took her son by the hand and left me by the water. I watched as they crossed the bridge to join the community of onlookers on the other side.

What an amazing thing for her to say. What an amazing concept to take with me before I floated away into perhaps the greatest journey of my life.

Make a wish...

I wished that I didn't have to worry about my disease coming back, to finish what it started in Utah.

I wished I didn't have to live in constant pain.

I wished that I was stronger than my depression.

No... I could do better. Leave the melancholy behind. This wasn't the time or place for self-loathing and pity.

So instead, I wished that by the time I reached the Gulf, my life will have transformed beyond my wildest dreams.

I zipped up my rain jacket, tightened the drawstring on my wide-brimmed straw hat and climbed on my SUP. My father stood waving proudly from a crowd of clicking cameras and cell phones. After a final wave, I stood up on Old Blue and paddled away.

I believed the river was going to lead me to places I could never imagine. Not only through physical landscapes, but into new chapters of my life that would not exist without it.

There was no doubt in my mind.

My whole life had led to that moment.

RIVER JOURNAL,
JUNE 7, 2011

The young man playing his acoustic guitar is good... good enough for me to drift, at least. Relaxing by my gate, head on backpack, waiting to board the plane, it all hits me at once. i seldom think things through. i get an idea in my brain and jump headfirst before i can change my mind. inevitably, i succumb to panic at the last minute. i've really hyped this thing up and now i'm going to be on my favorite talk radio show, The Monster in the Morning on Real Radio 104.1. What if i don't finish? My ideas are always better than my reality.

2

Standing Up

I like to think there are reasons behind everything we do. Before an action, there are motivating factors that ignite the action in the first place. Maybe they are obvious, or perhaps they simply exist on a subconscious level. Whatever the case, there is sure to be a heartbeat behind the life of an idea; that blood pumping instigator that will not allow a peaceful night of sleep until the decision is made to relinquish control and surrender to the calling.

I suspect that early explorers were fueled by a variety of motivations: Greed, fame, the call of the wild.

Robert Cavelier de La Salle, a French explorer, was fueled by the desire to bring glory to France when he and his crew of eighteen Native Americans became the first documented explorers to navigate the length of the Mississippi in 1682.

Since the days of La Salle, countless others have braved the "Big Muddy" on a variety of vessels, from canoes to kayaks and even homemade rafts. People have long been exploring The Mighty's dark waters, steeped in a history of river pirates, voodoo, and sunken treasure. She captivated the imagination of Samuel Clemens, a.k.a. Mark Twain, who eventually penned some of my favorite childhood adventure stories like *The Adventures of Tom Sawyer* and *Huckleberry Finn.*

However, until the year 2012, in the sizzling month of June, nobody had ever attempted the expedition by stand-up paddleboard.

I was going to be that man.

I should be expected to follow such a claim with a detailed account of my extensive training and preparation. I could tell you that to take on such a remarkable endeavor requires a sound mind and peak physical condition. I could give testimony to the months spent incorporating free-weights and a grueling cardiovascular regimen, complete with yoga for optimal flexibility.

When I was not in the gym, I was in the water, paddling long distances while analyzing the mechanics of everyday life on the river, preparing myself for the monotony of countless ten-hour days on the Mississippi. This type of training was not only beneficial for my physical stamina, but for my mental endurance as well, which will most likely be the driving force that projects me to my final destination in New Orleans. It always comes down to a person's will. When stories are told of great accomplishments, the victorious claim, "When I had no more strength to give, my will kept me going."

As far as my equipment—it was top of the line. My paddleboard was designed to withstand extreme conditions and travel great distances. I'd spent hours retrofitting my gear to maximize ease and transport, not to mention velocity and the overall performance of my SUP. My camping equipment was compact and highly efficient. Every ounce was carefully considered to ensure I neither carried too much nor too little. It was a perfect balance of necessity and comfort. My mental faculties were spot-on and I was at the top of my game. I was truly a force to be reckoned with.

Sure. Sounds legit. Now for the truth. My preparations for this journey were even less impressive than the humble beginnings of the Mighty Mississippi. My equipment was sub-par. My clothes consisted of surf trunks, flip-flops, and a *Dumb and Dumber* T-shirt. I had a steel framed backpack and a sleeping bag wrapped in a garbage bag. Old Blue was bottom shelf equipment. The only type of environment it needed to endure was my fist slamming against the deck in frustration when my legs would crap out after only five minutes of paddling due to the intense pain. In fact, the only items in my arsenal substantial enough to endure the 2,400-mile journey were my one-man tent and a dry box used to protect my IPod.

My physical condition was even worse than my equipment. I'd only been walking on my own for a few months. Before leaving Orlando for Minneapolis, I spent a few weeks on a river near my house with a 45lb Australian Shepherd on the bow and the rest of the time drinking beer. That was the extent of my preparation. There were no weights-no cardio. The morning after I purchased my plane ticket, I went into my garage, threw a backpack and sleeping bag on the deck of my SUP and tied a bungee cord around it. Done. I would have left the next day if it were possible.

The river was not about exploration for me at that time. It was about escape.

After my brush with the Reaper in 2010, I spent two months in a hospital bed fighting for my life and then another four months fighting to walk again. The last thing I was prepared for was the post-traumatic depression. When it came, I had nothing left to give. I would spend my days in bed drowning in depression and my nights at the neighborhood bar drowning in alcohol. I made promises that with the coming of each new dawn, I would take back my life, but then the physical pain would snuff out any motivation and another twenty-four hours would slip into the past.

I was desperate for a way to dilute the haunting memories of the hospital and the innocent mistake that had put me there. I couldn't shake them, and I was on my way to dying once more, but this time on an emotional level. So, in lieu of anti-depressants, I decided to paddleboard the fourth largest river in the world. There is a unique high that I get when making a decision to abandon my comfort zone. The further I venture, the deeper the rush.

My idea to SUP the Mississippi was not a well thoughtout plan. It came to fruition simply by one idea stumbling into another. While in my PTSD stupor, I would reminisce about my former life on the road. I needed my vagabond days. I pondered hiking the Appalachian Trail and I thought about doing some hitchhiking again. During a motorcycle trip on 2008, I read about a guy who canoed the entire length of the Mississippi and a river adventure intrigued me.

First seed planted...

The next was born of a lifetime love affair.

I've been in love with the water from the onset of memory. A Borders bookstore in my hometown of Altamonte Springs, Florida, was having a going out of business sale. It was there that I bought my first issue of *Stand Up Journal* and discovered the most meditative and exhilarating way to walk on water since the day my big brother Mark gave me his old surfboard when I was twelve.

The SUP brought me back to my great love for the first time since "the incident" occurred. Having been a surfer for most of my life, I was desperate to return to the ocean but I was still too weak. If I fell on a wave, I would most likely drown in the surf. Not only did I not have the upper body strength that I was accustomed to, but also, the damage to my lungs would inhibit my ability to hold my breath. There was still more rehabilitating to do. With the help of a new SUP and a small river near my house, I knew it wouldn't be long.

I hobbled home and showed my family pictures of people taking their SUP's through rivers, lakes and oceans, passing through some of the most magnificent landscapes with nothing more than four inches of foam and epoxy separating them from the elements. My parents wanted to help me continue my rehabilitation so they bought my first SUP.

Second seed planted. They need only meet.

My first attempt at using my new paddleboard was less than encouraging. I tied my SUP to the bed of my Dodge and drove down to the Wekiva Marina. The Wekiva is a spring-fed river that flows through the suburbs like a streak of history in a modern world. In the Muscogee language (also known as Creek; spoken by the Creek and Seminole Indians) Wekiva means "spring of water." Originally inhabited by the Timucuan Indians, the river winds itself for fifteen plus miles, through a lush ecosystem of Florida forest and mangrove, before spilling into the St. Johns River.

I lasted five minutes on the Wekiva before my legs caught fire in agonizing pain. It was like my heart was pumping muriatic acid through my veins instead of blood. I paddled back to the dock and cried into my hands for five minutes then stood up and tried it again.

In the days that followed, I paddled fifteen minutes, then twenty, and so on, until it was enjoyable. The water was cool and clear and it made me happy... if only for a moment. Sometimes I would lie flat on my board and watch the sky trickle through the emerald canopy, spilling droplets of light. When the woods gave way to open spaces, the sun would consume me and ignite my life.

It was on the Wekiva that my lust for adventure began to stir once more. I dreamed through the day, floating in the quiet, amongst tree and sky. How far could a person go on a paddleboard? How far has someone already gone? As I paddled, my head would clear just enough for me to hear the voice again—that same voice that came to me in the coma. It was quiet at first: *Pay it forward*, and it grew louder the longer I paddled, causing me to feel anxious. *Use what happened to bring hope to another.* The very idea that I could bring hope to anyone was ridiculous.

How can the hopeless bring hope?

While in the water, I existed once more, but after my session was finished, lifelessness returned before I could load my paddleboard back into the truck. I realize how strange it must sound for a person to experience such emotional darkness after receiving the gift of a second chance. You would expect to feel nothing less than thankfulness for every new breath. The mind/body connection is a beautiful thing; until something is out of balance, then it's nothing short of a nightmare.

The sadness wasn't there when I left the hospital. There is a picture of me sitting by the curb in my wheelchair, waiting for my dad to bring the car around. After a two-month stay in two different hospitals in two different states, I was finally coming home. I looked into the hazy Florida sun, closed my eyes, and let the rays bathe me in peace. You could see it on my face as my mom snapped the photo.

The depression fell upon me gradually, but once it took hold, it smothered me in tar-like darkness. I used fermented hops and barley to wash away the guilty feelings I had for not living how everyone expects a survivor to live. It helped to blur images and dull memories of horrid, dirty things, but somehow they always returned. There is no erasing the past. People say it's possible, but I don't believe it. You're never free from some things. Some cuts are too deep, and they leave puffy pink scars with jagged edges. But giving up was never an option. Even if the body and mind falter, the spirit survives and by simply hanging on, putting one foot before the other. Life can take a dramatic turn for the beautiful when we least expect it. Ideas can strike in the darkest of hours. The idea for a paddleboard adventure eventually pieced itself together on a steamy summer day after another sad attempt to acclimate my broken body to my new SUP.

Thunder rumbled in the distance, signaling the passing of yet another sporadic Florida thunderstorm. Lingering drops of rain trickled through the treetops and drip dropped to the river below, causing an almost inaudible hiss as the tepid tears made contact with the year-round, seventy-four degree, spring-fed waters of the Wekiva.

I sat on the edge of the dock with one foot anchoring my SUP to keep it from floating away while fiercely massaging the other, doing my best to alleviate the waves of static pain that ran from toe to hip.

Goeasyonyourselfgoeasyonyourselfgoeasyonyourself.

Like a broken record, they echoed in my head. My family. The doctors.

"Don't push too hard. You almost died just nine months ago."

So what...

"You shouldn't make any life altering decisions for at least a year."

Too late. My life has been altered beyond recognition.

I breathed in the steamy post-storm humidity and exhaled before standing up on my paddleboard for another round. I used my paddle to push off the dock and back into the lazy channel. Immediately, my feet began to swell and throb as if they had their own heartbeat. I paddled downstream for five minutes then fought the current back and found rest on the dock once more. I was done.

I tried to hide my struggle as I pulled the SUP from the water and dragged it towards my truck. People noticed. It made me self-conscious. I hated how pathetic I looked. It felt like I was carrying a tree trunk under my arm and the veins in my neck were ripe and popping. Ten more steps to my truck, my grip gave out and my board slipped from my fingers, making a sickening crunch as the epoxy rail collided with concrete. I wove a fine tapestry of obscenities, (If there wasn't already a crowd watching, there was now), threw my board in the back of my truck and collapsed on the tailgate.

After a short rest, I secured my SUP, climbed into the driver's seat and turned the key. I was about to shift into reverse when I caught my reflection in the rearview mirror. The setting sun flashed crimson rays through my dusty windshield, igniting my eyes and honing them into pale blue flames. Tears pooled in the corners. I did my best to contain them. Eventually, they spilled over the sunbaked lines on my cheeks and for the first time since the onset of the disease, I allowed myself to mourn. I sat, heaving tears into the palms of my hands, thanking a God, who I had never met, for sparing my life, and begging a God, who I'd never heard speak, for the strength to live again. I couldn't change what had happened to me. I couldn't change what I would have to endure for the rest of my life, but I could change how I was dealing with it. I wanted to take the horrors of what happened and pair it with a remarkable journey, creating the potential to bring hope to others.

Those two seeds converged that day. One planted while on a motorcycle trip and the other with the purchase of a new SUP. They took root and I all I needed to do was add water.

Could I physically do it with my "new" sick body?

Did I have the courage?

I wiped my swollen red eyes and picked up the copy of *Stand Up Journal* resting on the dashboard. I thumbed through the pages as I had done every day since I bought it and my mind began to piece together subconscious ramblings into coherent thoughts. My desire for another great adventure made me think of my motorcycle trip, which led to me to remembering about the man who canoed the Mississippi, which caused me to ponder the possibilities of great distances on a SUP.

And there it was. The question, the question that would change my life forever.

Has anyone ever SUP'ed the Mississippi?

At that moment, a decision was made. I had a plane to catch.

River Journal,
June 10, 2011

Though the Minnesota skies are
gray, my soul is bursting with
vibrant shades of greens and
blues. My body is still so very
weak but there is something
inside of me creating strength
and confidence. i've passed
through the initial panic that
surfaced from jumping headfirst
into this adventure and now i
feel nothing but excitement. i
am about to embark on a mighty
journey...

3

10 Hours on the Mississippi

The Mississippi River is the fourth longest river and the tenth largest river in the world. I would paddle past the borders of 10 states: Minnesota, Wisconsin, Iowa, Illinois, Missouri, Kentucky, Tennessee, and Louisiana, before reaching my journey's end.

There are conflicting calculations as to the actual length, but they range between 2,552 miles and 2,350 miles. Either way, it's a hell of a long paddle. To save the hassle, I'll refer to it as a 2,400 mile paddle and leave it at that.

Until recently, I didn't know anything about the Mississippi except from what I learned from Tom Sawyer and Huckleberry Finn.

I knew she was muddy and extensive. I've probably crossed The Mighty a dozen times in my life without so much as a glance, but now we were about to become more intimate than any other geographical landmark I had ever encountered.

It came as no surprise that the greatest journey of my life would be on the water. It was inevitable. I've been attracted to water since I could walk. Probably before. Whether it be streams, rivers, or creeks, if it was moving, I was either in it, around it, or floating homemade leaf-boats down it. There's something about dry ground falling into the liquid realm— the solid meeting the fluid—that kept me coming back. I'm more comfortable in the water than on dry land.

I learned to surf in New Smyrna Beach, Florida. The break was about an hour from our house. I wasn't old enough to drive, so opportunities to surf were sporadic. I struggled for months graduating from standing up to actually riding the whitewater straight into shore. This uneventful form of surfing went on for another several months and then, on a poetically bright summer day, I caught a clean face and took my surfing to the next level. My drop-in was flawless. A wall of water formed ahead of me and I rode parallel to shore cradled in the blue-green energy. It was the single most exhilarating moment of my young life, and it remains a memory I retreat to often when times are difficult. I think I ran over a couple of angry locals but all I can remember was my beating heart and the smile on my face.

I would cling to water in times of trouble. Whenever my mind would run rampant, I could always count on the methodical hum that came from being under water to put me at ease. It didn't matter what I was doing: surfing, snorkeling, sailing, or swimming, if I was in the water, I was happy, and I was certain that today would be no exception.

Fifteen minutes after my launch from the headwaters, the sun began to poke its way through the gloomy gray clouds like spaghetti through a strainer. It was still chilly, but nice, and I was full of hope. Nothing could bring me down. I kept pumping my ego, relishing in my minimal accomplishments, which I thought were impressive. I'm a great adventurer! I covered the country for a year on a motorcycle. I lived on a sailboat in the Pacific Ocean. I beat death. Conquering the Mighty Mississippi would be as easy as navigating the Wekiva River back home. I endured six months of helplessness. But today, at the start of my ultimate adventure, I was a confident explorer once more, insulated in a thick layer of arrogance.

I floated on my knees for the first few hundred yards, due to the low-lying tree branches, and then began to test my river legs, standing upright whenever the canopy would allow. Old Blue was dragging and his rails were deeper in the water than I would have liked. Nagging thoughts of poor preparation began to creep in, but I forced them out. First day growing pains was all it was, I told myself. Sometimes, the river would turn so sharply on itself, the nose of my paddleboard would catch the bank, and the current would push my tail against the opposite shore and wedge me in.

The Mighty was born in shallow waters. I had to remove my fin because it would snag on broken branches hidden beneath the surface and attempt to catapult me headfirst into the cold water. Though I anticipated harmony, it wasn't long before I realized that the Mississippi would not flow easily into my arms without a fight.

I spent the first two hours standing up, sitting down, standing up, sitting down, just to avoid fallen trees and debris blocking the river. There was no way to know what lie waiting around every turn, but my river maps from the Department of Natural Resources (DNR) were well marked and would at least alert me to some potential hazards, such as rapids, culverts and dams. The first obstacle marked on my map was a culvert. A culvert is a tunnel that allows the river to flow under roadways. As the river increases in width, bridges take the place of culverts. The map suggested porting around, but I remembered reading that kayakers paddled through them. This particular one was about fifty feet long and no more than thirty-six inches in diameter. I laid flat on my board, tucked in my arms, and shot through like a water slide, giggling as I splashed out the other side.

The river continued to wind like a snake through the woods and into open fields of tall grass. I saw beavers swimming, flat iron tails waving goodbye before disappearing under the surface. My board was so quiet that sometimes I would sneak up on white-tailed deer. I'd stand completely still and let the current carry me close. They would sense my presence and for a fleeting moment, we'd make eye contact then I'd watch them bounce away and vanish into the landscape. It was a beautiful start of what I anticipated to be the most spectacular and grueling journey of my life. I imagined those beautiful first moments would last through every mile that lie ahead and I was going to see it through to the end no matter what.

And then it happened.

It was early afternoon when the tall grass gave way to the forest. The scenery was beautiful. It was like paddling through Middle Earth. I sat down on my board for a breather, swallowed a handful of trail mix, and quenched my thirst with a tug at my water bottle. That's when I noticed the river had quickened its pace beneath me. I could hear gushing and gurgling ahead. Rapids were approaching. Not big ones, but rapids mean rocks, and rocks do not mix well with paddleboards. I remembered rapids were marked on the DNR maps, and there was supposed to be a place to portage on the left bank but during my emotional bliss, chomping on nuts and raisins, I missed it.

I began to calculate an exit strategy. I took my eyes off the river for a brief moment, and that's all it took. My board went from forward motion to a violent halt, launching me headfirst into cold water. My back struck rock with a paralyzing thud. I was stuck in the rapids, head pointed downriver, as the water rushed over my body, filling my mouth and nose. I struggled to pull up and free myself from the strap around my ankle, but my core was not strong enough. The water engulfed me with its frigid liquid. I mustered what strength I had, lunged forward, and managed to grab hold of my leash, freeing myself from its hold. The strap securing my gear to Old Blue broke and my packs spilled into the rapids. I reached out to grab them while still clinging to a rock. Once I claimed lord over my legs, I was able to throw my waterlogged gear to shore and wade through the rapids to free my paddleboard that was pin-balling off the jagged rocks.

With all items accounted for, I stumbled to shore and collapsed, trying to figure out what had just happened. I cursed my stupidity while choking down an energy bar. "What's wrong with you? Who wears a leash on a paddleboard, floating down the river? This isn't the ocean, dumb ass!" My skin was stinging. I looked down and gasped at the sight of the speckled black plague that consumed my arms and legs. Mosquitoes the size of grapes swarmed about my head and landed on every square inch of exposed skin. I could not sit for more than five seconds before becoming completely covered. I jumped to my feet and did a *getthehelloffme* dance. A thought came to me that maybe I was smart enough to stash repellant in my easily accessible camel pack and I was relieved to find that I had. It didn't mask the failure, but I felt a little better that I anticipated something important. I sprayed my body down and dropped to my knees in relief. It was then that I caught sight of Old Blue.

In all the chaos, I never noticed my board when I pulled it from the river. The bottom was Swiss cheese—at least thirty puncture wounds from bobbing on the rocks. The scene brought tears to my eyes. I picked him up out of the mud and gently laid him across my lap. My board was special to me. I felt like I was holding my best friend on the battlefield after the enemy had riddled him with bullets. I dressed his wounds with duct tape, (it was the best I could do), and apologized for the beating he just took because of my carelessness.

How my beautiful union with nature could turn into such a bitch-slap in a matter of seconds kept me in a state of disbelief for another fifteen minutes until the repellant began to wear off my wet skin, giving the blood-suckers permission to violate me all over again. I had to move. I couldn't sit in the desolate woods forever. I scarfed down yet another energy bar and got back in the water, still determined to conquer. My gear was now twice as heavy, allowing water to lap over the surface of my SUP. It was no longer a silky smooth glide across the surface, but a strenuous fight to move forward with every stroke of the paddle. The initial cold and adrenaline helped to numb the pain in my back, but as the fourth hour approached, the sciatic nerve down my left leg started throbbing. By the sixth hour, I was struggling to stand and could barely pull my saturated board down river.

The first campsite downriver form the headwaters was Coffee Pot Landing. I had circled it on my maps earlier that day, but it was still miles away, and I feared I would not reach my destination before dark. Nothing came easy; not one inch. When I'd hit a narrow cutback in the river, my board would snag and I had to drop into the cold water and turn it by hand. The tall grass returned—an endless floating bog, too spongy to walk on or rest. The rails of my board were under water, and because the river remained shallow, I couldn't put my fin on so it was a constant struggle just to keep it straight. My back and leg seared with pain. I was cold, wet, and humiliated. There were brief moments that I'd start to warm back up again, but then I'd lose my balance from pain and exhaustion and plunge back into the water.

There was no sun, no relief, and I was completely alone.

That's when I felt the first drop on my cheek.

I closed my eyes, "Please... no."

Another drop and another one still, until the rain fell in unison. I dropped my paddle to my side and hung my head. Rain mixed with the cold Mississippi dripped from my eyes. I so desperately wanted to be home again, lying in my warm bed in a depressed stupor, waiting for happy hour. My depression was an excuse to sleep, drink, and pop antidepressants. It was easy. I wanted it back but most of all, I wanted off the river.

My gear was soaked and bloated due to my lack of proper preparation, my board had holes in it, and my body was crying out for mercy. Thanks to my disease, the joints in my ankles, elbows, and wrists were on fire and the medicine I had to take every day to keep the illness from raiding my body caused painful stomach cramping.

By my eighth hour on the Mighty, I went from a confident adventurer to a babbling idiot. Inches felt like miles as I crept down the winding river. I prayed to God... I begged the Great Spirit and bargained with Buddha to help me find Coffee Pot Landing before dark. As dusk approached, my hope began to fade. There was no place to stop because the grass refused to provide stable ground. Eventually, the sun disappeared and I found myself stranded in the gray space before darkness.

It was in that final hour of panic and despair that I noticed the power lines. I knew from my map that Coffee Pot Landing was a river mile from this particular landmark and it gave me the boost I needed to continue. That last hour of my first day will be sewn into my subconscious forever. When I finally reached the campground ten hours later, I was done. It was over. And I was going home.

I struggled to pull my SUP and gear to shore before collapsing in the mud. I felt like a cocky boxer KO'd for the first time in his career. I rolled over on my back and stared into the sky while mosquitoes buzzed in my ears. How could something so wonderful and exciting turn into such a nightmare? As I lay in the mud, I struggled to keep the pressures of failure from breaking me apart. I was unsure how badly my back was injured, but even worse than the pain was the feeling that had I let myself down along with the people I cared about.

I managed to crawl up the bank, taking several excruciating trips to get my gear out of the water. I even set up my tent because some crazy part of me was still refusing to quit. Everything was soaked, including my sleeping bag. Mosquitoes engulfed my face. My cold trembling hands fumbled for my phone, only to find there was no service. Out in the distance, beyond the woods, I could hear the hum of what I assumed were passing cars, so I left my gear behind and limped in the general direction hoping to find a road. A half-mile later, I hit concrete, but there was still no cell service, so I kept walking. I hadn't gone more than a hundred yards when I saw a car pull out of the woods in front of me.

The car pulled up and an older woman with a kind face poked her head out of the driver's side window. I was not the first injured river man Sheryl Riggs had seen limping past her farm.

"Are you hurt?" Sheryl asked.

"Yes…" I moaned, "My back." I didn't take time to explain what I was doing just yet. "I need to call my dad. I think he's still nearby but I don't have service."

"My property is right here. Get in and I'll take you to my house so you can use the phone."

I'd met several gracious and kind people in Minnesota in a short time, but Sheryl and her daughter Cori will always be two of my favorites. They brought me into their home, gave me aspirin and a drink, and helped me reach my dad. Cori's four-year-old son, Max, put a Dora Band-Aid on my hand and then stood up on the chair next to me and shoved a homemade cookie into my mouth. I shared my story with them and my colossal failure to which Sheryl replied, "You should be proud that you even made the attempt."

It was a kind thing to say, but I was not proud in the slightest.

An hour later, my dad picked me up at the Riggs' residence. He was supposed to be in Minneapolis, but decided to stay another day to be sure I was moving safely downstream. I limped to the car, buried my face in my hands, and broke down.

I led him back to Coffee Pot so we could retrieve my gear and we traveled silently back to Park Rapids, except for a few encouraging words from my dad. They were similar to what Sheryl had said, like, it was brave of me to even attempt such a thing, especially in my condition. I didn't listen. I anguished the thought of coming home after just one day, but I was completely broken in body and in spirit, and there was no way in hell I was getting back on that river.

The van hummed quietly down the dark wooded highway and the further from the river we rolled, the more comfortable I was in my decision to go home. I asked my dad to buy me a plane ticket so I could return with him. I would give him the cash I had to run the river and then put this entire irrational impulse behind me.

Nobody needs my story.

RIVER JOURNAL,
JUNE 11, 2011

A dream begins and a dream ends. i'm coming home. What an embarrassing failure. it's all i can do to type this entry when what i really want to do is hurl my computer through the hotel window, along with my body, but my room is on the first floor which would result in another humiliating defeat. i'm torn between the overwhelming desire to get out of Minnesota and return home to my warm familiar bed and the soul-ravaging agony of defeat. i was unprepared-mentally, emotionally and physically. and i paid the price.

4

Over Troubled Waters

My sleep pulsed with dark, uneasy dreams.

I clawed and kicked at my blankets searching for comfort, but physical comfort is impossible when mentally struggling deep within. I stared at the ceiling while a slide show of memories passed through my head. There have been many times throughout my life where my shortcomings have stolen my smile and drenched my soul in fear. My first inclination after a failure or an unforeseen calamity is to close off the world and wallow in doubt. I tried to tell myself it would be fine if I went home because I was still a very sick man who was in over his head, but no matter what excuses I cultivated, I knew I would kick myself for the rest of my life for quitting. If I went home, I would never make the same attempt again.

I don't like being afraid. In fact, I loathe it. My dad knew this about me as well. That's why he never bought me a ticket home. In the morning, there was a knock at my hotel room door. I opened it to see my dad standing there with hot coffee. He smiled when he saw the look in my eye. He knew what I was thinking. He asked me a question, but it was more of a statement.

"You're not going home, are you…?"

"No. But I have no idea how I'm going to get back on that river."

I can describe my dad in a variety ways, but what he said next sums up his character the way I know him best.

"Son, if you want to give it another shot, I will help you figure it out."

So that's what we did. We figured it out. He could have lectured me on my failed attempts at proper preparation. It was obvious that taking on a quest as massive as paddle boarding America from top to bottom requires more than three weeks of planning, but no such words were spoken.

Only, "I will help you figure it out."

It's hard to isolate the reasons behind my decision to continue, but when morning came, and the sun shone bright and warm, I was ready to get wet. Maybe I was tired of the broken man I morphed into after the hospital and wanted to feel like myself again. Whatever it was, I went to bed a quitter and when I woke, nothing could keep me from returning to the river. I had been measured, weighed and found wanting... but I didn't have to accept it.

I learned some humbling lessons that first ten hours on the Mississippi river, but two stand above the rest.

First: No great thing is accomplished on our own. To be part of something spectacular takes a team. I always think I'm alone. I expect to be alone, but I'm not. I possess a stubborn, unwillingness to quit, but it was my dad, standing by me, that ensured my journey would continue.

Second: You can fight against nature and get hurt or you can listen and survive. I thought I knew something of adventure and then I was given a 10-hour lesson on how little I know of self-reliance and how quickly things can go wrong. That may be the worst of the river or it may have been the best. The question is not, and never should be, "How do I conquer the river?" I should learn to flow with it, take whatever it sends my way, and turn it into a successful cohabitation for the next few months, and if unity is unattainable... how do I successfully adapt and survive? My dad left me alone and went to secure our room for a couple more days. I limped into the bathroom and splashed cold water on my face. Every muscle ached and my leg throbbed like it had its own heartbeat, but when I looked into the mirror my grin was back. I call it my *Indiana Jones grin*. He got that smirk whenever he was getting his ass kicked or landed himself in a situation that was sure to end him. Then he would grin as if to say, "Do your worst, for I'm sure to do mine."

I wanted to raise money for the hospital and pay forward the generosity I had received a year ago while knocking on death's door. I wanted to make my family and friends proud, and sure, I wanted to set a world record, but it was no longer about any of those things at the moment. My head was in the game. It was about me, the river, and the enduring question... "What am I really made of?"

Dad and I spent the next two days forging me into a lean, mean, paddling machine. I dumped the comforts of home from my pack and took only what was necessary to survive. The medicine I take that keeps my sarcoidosis from eating me alive weighed almost ten pounds alone and every ounce counts on a paddleboard. I went from fifty pounds of gear to maybe thirty-five, give or take, which was significant. We upgraded my backpack and put everything in dry sacks so if I were to take another spill, my belongings would stay dry, and then I went to work patching over thirty holes in Old Blue with marine grade epoxy.

After all preparations were complete for my comeback, my dad and I enjoyed some down time together. There wasn't much to do in the quiet little town of Park Rapids, but we could always sniff out a movie theater. We found a small cinema no bigger than a two car garage adorned in crimson red curtains and sank into the worn red seats. I think we saw *Super 8*.

It's because of my dad that I am such an avid movie buff. I'll never forget the first movie we saw together. Maybe he's to blame for my adventurous spirit and perpetual wanderlust because of what he exposed me to in the early days of my youth.

I'm talking about Mexico and Indiana Jones.

ooo

The year was 1981. I was eight-years old when my dad took me to see *Raiders of the Lost Ark*. I'm sure there were a few theater experiences prior, but I don't remember them. In my heart, my love for movies started with Indiana Jones.

The next day, I rummaged through my closet for anything resembling his now legendary ensemble. I found a white short-sleeve button-down shirt, that in no way resembled Indy's, and a pair of khakis with a hole in the crotch. Close enough.

In the end, my uniform consisted of pleated khakis, white shirt, and a nylon rope tied to a stick, posing as a whip, that clung to my belt with fishing line. I did with what I had. I was going to be Indiana Jones and lack of authenticity would not stop me. But I would be lying if I didn't confess my aching desire for the holy trinity of adventure accessories: A hat, a shoulder bag, and a real leather whip.

However crude my costume was, it would not stay that way, and the unique circumstances in which my missing pieces found one another, and the miles they traveled to complete a young boy's transformation into that of globetrotting hero, is worth a recounting.

A few months following the ultimate in cinematic experiences, my dad took me on a mission trip to Mexico. He was a pastor for the Seventh-Day Adventist Church, and in his younger years, he would take trips to places like Haiti and Mexico to help build schools and churches—a tradition the two of us share today through a non-profit we organized together, working with the public schools in Costa Rica. It was in Mexico that I would acquire a most sacred piece in my Indy arsenal.

My first twelve hours in Mexico planted a wanderlust deep within me that has remained unquenchable to this day. We flew into Mexico City and it was chaos the moment I stepped off the plane with all the buzzing, beeping cars and foreign tongues. Before leaving the city to begin our final leg of the journey by bus, we stopped at a grocery store for some necessities. As I wandered the cereal aisle, I saw a boy pissing on the floor near the *Frutti Aros* (Froot Loops) and the *Zucaritas* (Frosted Flakes). Welcome to nowhere like home, Matt.

The majority of our week was spent toiling under the dry flames of the Aztec sun. I carried concrete blocks and my dad laid them in place. We slept in tents and I'd talk until I heard him start to snore and then I would drift off into the type of sleep that will always belong to that first adventure and will never return again.

After the work portion of our mission was over, the group took a day for sightseeing and souvenir shopping before returning home the following morning. I'm not sure what got into my dad that day, but we loaded our bags with pottery, marionettes, swords with eagle heads on the handle, (which came in small, medium, and large blades and we bought all three) and a sombrero that a family could have used for shelter. Somewhere in the midst of our overdose on Mexican collectables, I spotted the whip hanging from a hook, nailed to a post, inside a souvenir shop. A real life, made of leather, snap-popping bullwhip. I was certainly too young to know what an orgasm was, but what I experienced as I softly ran my fingertips down her leather-woven outline had to be damn near close to one.

My dad bought me three of them.

I will always remember Mexico for her sights, smells, children peeing in supermarkets and my precious bullwhips.

We returned from Mexico and, a few months later, my parents finally got around to taking their honeymoon (twelve years after they were married). After years of saving, they went to Europe, and it was in Venice that my mom found me a leather bag and a Fedora. The trifecta was complete.

I goofed around in our little yard back home, digging holes, burying treasures, and wrapping my new whip around anything and everything. However, my first real adventure in full Indy attire did not happen until our annual trip to my grandparents' house in Nashville the following summer. Yards back home were a thumbtack compared to the ones in my Granny's neighborhood. Behind her house and the surrounding homes, was a cluster of woods that concealed a nice little creek. It was prime real estate for adventure. After a hearty breakfast, which included a choice of brightly colored sugar cereals (which were strictly prohibited back home), I sprang from the table, through the back door, and sprinted across the backyard adorned in my hero's armor, ready to face rolling boulders, slithering snakes, and a giant bald-headed Nazi waiting to fight me for my treasure.

If I were to return to those woods today, I'm sure they would feel cramped compared to my memory of them. However, in those days my imagination was a bit out of the ordinary, and by the time I was ten paces in, the woods gave way to the vibrant emerald canopy of the Amazon, perspiring with exotic life. An ancient Amazonian tribe was after me and the treasure I possessed. I raced along the creek bed, hopping logs and dodging spider webs in attempts to lose my imaginary pursuers. There was no more reality... only fantasy. The forest was foreign ground, and with every stride, I fell deeper into character. It was total kid ecstasy. I had no fear of the woods nor being alone in them.

That was about to change.

I don't know how long it had been or how far I was from my grandparents' house, but eventually the woods spilled into a clearing, exposing the gentle upward slope of a neighboring yard where a woman sat in her lawn chair approximately 100 yards away. Two brawny German Shepherds, who were alert to my presence before I even knew they existed, stood guard next to their owner.

In real time, they were fast. In "oh crap I'm gonna die" time, they traveled at the speed of light. I froze, enveloped in a fear unlike anything I had ever experienced in my juvenile existence. I heard the woman scream which helped to loosen the chains that bound my instincts and I turned to run. I was successful at a twenty-yard sprint before the jungle hounds caught me in their protective rage. The first shepherd rammed into the back of my legs just as the second sunk a canine below my right shoulder blade. They had me pinned to the ground, my neck in line with their powerful jaws. There was no concept of time, only searing pain and the sonic crack of a dog's bark breaking air a few inches from my face. The owner must have been close behind, because as quickly as the terror began it ended in a jolt. She was hysterical. She cradled me, pressing her hand against the wound in my back. I could feel the wetness between my shirt and skin. It was sticky and warm.

Everything after that moment, lying in her arms, was lost somewhere in my memory's memory. I don't know how I got from the woods to the hospital, but I'll never forget my shirt. It sat next to me on the examining table, the back completely covered in dried blood. The doctor told me I was a lucky boy; a few centimeters over and I would've had a punctured lung.

My mom brought me back to my grandparents' house where my family doted on me, trying to comfort me. My older brother Mark chimed in with a smart-ass, "How come you didn't use your whip?" It was funny, but I wasn't in the mood for jokes. My mom assured me that all of my sacred gear was present and accounted for (minus one bloody shirt) and ready for more adventure, but I didn't care. My spirit was broken. Fear was already spreading, rapidly infecting my desire for further adventures. As far as I was concerned, there was no way in hell I was ever going back in the woods.

Sound familiar?

There's a definable parallel between my experiences with the vicious jungle hounds and my first day on the river, along with every other failure from that day to this. And my dad was there on the other side of every one. When I hung my head in defeat, he was always there to raise it back up.

"Son, you're not a failure as long as you never quit. And even if you do, it's still not over. You can choose to get up and try again."

His words have been a lighthouse behind every harsh storm that I've had to face.

There is no life without troubled waters. Try to avoid them if you'd like, and let me know if you figure out the secret to a pain-free existence. The only relief I've found comes in the form of a bridge. It can be a parent, a lover, or a complete stranger placed in your life at the exact moment you needed them most. Each one can have a profound impact if you are open to a learning experience.

A bridge over troubled water—that's what my father is to me. He is the man I hope to become one day, but I fear I will never come close. His quiet humility and constant support have been the rock on which I have anchored on many occasions. This is not to say that I don't have an equally amazing mother. I most certainly do. She's the one that told him not to leave my side no matter how long it took until I was comfortable with the Mighty. However, for immediate purposes, this was about my dad. The sole reason I was getting back on the river.

Two days had passed since my initial launch. It was time for rebirth. There are several memories in my life that I can recall with vibrancy; the moment I pushed off the bank at Coffee Pot Landing on my second attempt at the Mighty Miss will always be one of them.

It was chilly and blue. I took no gear with me. My dad kept it in the van. This was about getting back on the river and putting my failure behind me... and that's what I did. He wanted to take me to an easier launch site, but I was not going to cheat... not one inch. It was back into my moment of hell or no place at all.

I felt some tension during that first hour. I was a bit jumpy, hoping to avoid another mishap, but after five miles, I was back in the game and enjoying the twinge of confidence that was returning. Thinking about failure would not benefit my journey, so I focused on the beauty around me and evaporated into the moment. The sky, the trees, the clear cool water. The freedom that comes from a river adventure is like no other.

The morning consisted of more grass and miles of it. Eventually, the foliage broke apart into a series of ponds dotting a land mass as large as several football fields. I entered the first pond, then another, and yet another, and it wasn't long before I found myself in trouble once more. As I moved from pond to pond, I lost the main channel and corralled myself into the marsh. I circled the small chain of ponds, and found nothing but more dead ends at every turn. The headwinds were so strong that it blew the surface water in different directions. I began retracing my steps only to dig myself deeper into my dilemma. I could see dry land from where I was paddling but couldn't get to it; the marsh separating the lakes was too spongy to walk on, and just high enough to keep my line of sight from finding a discernible channel. It was a frustrating sixty minutes. My anger began to boil as old demons surfaced. I decided to sit down and have a snack, hoping that if I removed myself from the situation a solution would prevent itself. But before I could sit, I noticed, off in the distance about fifty yards away, two heads floating in the reeds.

I paddled towards the oddity and that's when I ran into Randy and Alex. They were in a canoe, so from my initial perspective, it looked as if their heads were floating above the marsh.

"Now that's the way to travel!" Randy called out as I approached.

"Right now I'm just going in circles! My name is Matt."

Randy lifted his hand, "I'm Randy. This is Alex." Alex waved.

"I've been paddling around the tall grass for an hour trying to find the channel," I said.

That's when Alex taught me another valuable lesson in nature that I would use often on my way downstream. He showed me that no matter what was happening on the surface, the undergrowth would always bow towards the rivers current. Sure enough, I looked down and the grass lay low in one direction even though the wind was blowing the opposite way. Proof that you can't always judge something by the surface.

Randy and Alex were teachers from Minneapolis who had always dreamed about taking a canoe from the headwaters back to the Twin Cities. I've always felt intoxicated by individuals who are living a dream. It's a pure form of happiness that's hard to rival. We spent the rest of the morning paddling alongside each other and the fellowship of strangers set to a Kinkade canvas was harmonious.

The river transitioned back into the forest. It was narrow in many parts and logs and trees blocked our path. I felt bad for the guys because they would have to empty their canoe and climb over while I was able to lay flat on my board and drift under fallen obstacles.

Our hours of talking and paddling moved into noontime and the teachers wanted a break, but I was rambling on. We made plans to hang out in Minneapolis but it never happened.

I was finding my river rhythm with each mile paddled. Challenges would present themselves and I would methodically overcome them and move on. There were places in the north country where the river was like liquid glass. I would paddle past schools of Rock Bass, hundreds of them, fat and juicy. I should have brought my fishing pole. This would have been Heaven for my little brother Jonathan. That kid fishes in his sleep. This, of course, led me to reminisce about life with my little brother. That's what solo adventures do to a person, if permitted. In the solitude, they force one to embrace all spectrums of his or her life, good and bad, past and present. Like everything else, my reflections usually leave me with a sadness that I could have done better.

For eight years, it was just Mark and me. My parents wanted another child, Jonathon arrived and the party of five was complete. I remember walking into the house after school and seeing him sleeping in his bassinet. He was family the moment I laid eyes on him. He was my baby brother. My blood.

As he grew, I was his hero and then I left him. I went to high school and on to adult life and never so much as looked back at him standing at the door each time I walked away. It wasn't intentional. I loved him then as I do now and I make it a point to see him as often as possible, but I know I left him with scars and it breaks my heart.

If only I could have a moment to go back and turn away from my adolescent activities and spend another day with my little brother, the child who saw me as his hero. But I have the now and the now is what's important.

I sat down on my SUP, cupped some cool water, and washed my puffy red eyes. Just a week on the Mighty and her waters were already flushing out my emotions. I turned my attention back to the bass. They fluttered wildly beneath my SUP and I tried to snatch them up with my hands like a bear but it wasn't going to happen. I grabbed a cord from my backpack, stuck a safety pin at the end, and skewered some beef jerky to it but that wasn't happening either. Eventually, I gave up efforts and pulled out my camera, hoping to get a shot of the frolicking fish, lost my grip, and watched it bounce off my board into the chilly water.

Before I floated past, I could see my camera at the bottom of the river, its shiny silver case sparkling amongst the evergreen reeds. It was waterproof up to a certain depth, so I knew it was still a perfectly functioning camera. I hesitated for a moment, weighing the options of plunging into the water against the current or simply floating on, leaving my camera to a watery grave. The river was cold and I was thoroughly annoyed at myself because I knew I was going to dive in after it, and would spend the next several hours wet and shivering, but I needed that camera.

My first attempt was pure comedy. I took some thin nylon rope from my pack and tied it to a low-lying branch then back down to my board. That way, when I dove in the water, Old Blue would not continue the trip without me. I paddled to where I was positioned directly above the camera and dove in headfirst, but I was six feet downriver by the time I reached the bottom. I allowed the current to float me back to Old Blue dangling from the end of his string. I climbed back on and paddled up river once more.

Taking what I learned from my first failed attempt, I paddled past the camera several feet hoping to outsmart the current, so that by the time I reached the bottom, I would find my precious Olympus firmly in my grasp.

Dive—Splash—Miss—"Dammit!"

Second attempt was closer. I actually grazed the camera with my fingertips, but no prize. My lips were turning blue and by the time I floated back to Old Blue, still waiting patiently at the end of his tether, I was in full-blown shivers. I had to laugh at the thought of someone watching this fool paddle upriver, dive into the water for no apparent reason, only to pop up cursing, teeth chattering and then repeat.

For my third attempt, I paddled a good ten feet upriver, past the camera. I dove strong for the bottom and swam against the swift undertow with my eyes wide open. There was a flash of silver and a frantic grasp. My fist broke the surface, camera clenched tightly, with my head close behind. I let out a triumphant roar.

I was so excited that I rescued my camera, I accidentally floated passed my SUP, still dangling on its line against the current, and had to pull myself back upriver using the reeds. Eventually, both the camera and I were safely aboard Old Blue and on our way once more.

The rest of the day flowed gracefully, one hour after another. Around mid-afternoon, I paddled near a group of people grilling, fishing, and simply enjoying the river. They called out, waved me over and invited me to join them for some the best hot dogs I've ever had. (Everything is the best after a long day on the river). They fixed me a plate and would not let me leave until I was stuffed. After eating and listening to my story, the youth group from Leech Lake signed my board (I brought a Sharpie with me so everyone I met could sign my paddleboard) and I pushed off the dock, waving farewell as I floated out of their lives. I was dry and warm thanks to the afternoon sun, and sufficiently fed, thanks to my new friends.

At the end of my second day, I managed to log in twenty-two miles; an accomplishment that brought some much needed pride back to my soul after the beating I took that first day. My body could still feel the pains from bouncing off the rapids like a ping-pong ball, but it was only physical discomfort and I'll take that over the mental ache of defeat any day of the week.

What a difference a day makes. I hoped to remember this the next time I found myself swimming in darkness.

Dad and I at the Headwaters.

Ready for float. Mississippi River Headwaters.

An interesting first day.

Dad and I at Tabor's Cabins. Bemidji, MN.

Tom and Charlotte Chatfield and friends

RIVER JOURNAL,
JUNE 18, 2011

Having my dad with me at
this time is something i will
cherish forever. it's been a long
time since we had such quality
interaction and i find myself,
on occasion, feeling sad about
the way time can so often slip
away from us, leaving us
feeling a bit guilty for not
appreciating the people in our
lives over the things in our lives.

5

The Two Lakes

I was relieved to find out at the end of my second day that my dad would not be leaving in the morning. He changed his plane ticket and made a commitment to stay by my side for the next two weeks so that I could test the new gear. At least that was one theory, but I had a suspicion that he had other reasons.

I'd add different components to the SUP each day, experimenting with different configurations to find the most efficient combinations of dry sacks and necessities. He also wanted to make sure that I was safely across Cass Lake and Lake Winnibigoshish, which would be two of the largest obstacles I would face in Minnesota.

Dad had a lot of time to kill during the day while I paddled, so he would meet people and talk to them about potential hazards down the river. Unanimously, the locals would speak of the two large lakes and give caution. Florida lakes are a dog dish compared to the lakes in Minnesota. My dad was feeling tense about my crossing because he knew them well; he grew up in Minnesota. He learned to drive a car on frozen lakes. Most of the stories I had heard growing up were of his childhood in

Minnesota, and some of them were about being on a boat when freak winds and capsizing waves would come out of nowhere.

I supposed helping me with the gear and making sure I was safe were acceptable theories, but at the end of the day, I think he just wanted to be with his son. The next two weeks with my dad will always be some of my most precious memories. The depression, pain and post-traumatic nightmares continued, so I worried that I was more of a chore to be around than a pleasant travel buddy, but he acted as if every minute with his boy was the best time of his life. As I paddled through the wilds of northern Minnesota into Bemidji, he stood at every bridge snapping photos and taking videos to post on my Facebook page and website. As I passed under each bridge, he dropped water and protein bars, and then followed his maps to the next overpass. In the evening, we would share a quiet meal and retire to whatever lodging he had secured during his scouting missions. One of our favorite places was Tabor's Cabins, located in Bemidji, home to Paul Bunyan and his blue ox Babe. Bemidji was deemed, "First city on the Mississippi." It was a great town full of good food and good people. Tabor's is home to cozy little chalets and it's worth checking out if you find yourself in wandering the wilds of Northern Minnesota and want to do some fishing.

It was at Tabor's Cabins that I began preparations for the big lakes.

I anticipated that Cass and Winnie would be relatively easy to navigate. It's basically a straight shot. I had, what I considered, a sufficient amount of practice by successfully paddling through a couple of smaller lakes, starting with Lake Bemidji. The river skirted the ends of Wolf Lake and Andrusia Lake, both of which were smooth sailing. The only misshap I encountered was my fin falling off in the middle of Lake Bemidji. I knew this by the immediate fishtailing. My dad managed to locate a sports shop about an hour away that actually carried SUP fins, and returned with a new one before I finished my day's paddle. Cass Lake, the smaller of the two, would be first at bat. Cass is the eleventh largest lake in Minnesota at around 15,000 acres. It was once considered the headwaters of the Mississippi in 1820 after an expedition led by the governor of Michigan, Lewis Cass. My route through the center would take me just shy of ten miles before I found the river's channel again.

The morning of my first attempt was foggy, and I noticed a strong breeze in the air, but paid no attention. My dad drove to the boat ramp off Mission Road where he picked me up the day before and I paddled through the channel into Alien Bay before making my way into Cass. The moment I passed through the strait into Cass Lake, strong headwinds pummeled me like an NFL linebacker. I would pull my paddle through the water and by the time I brought it forward for another stroke, the wind had pushed me back a foot. I managed to gain 50 yards in an hour before I was plucked from the lake, exhausted, by yet another good Samaritan, Marlow and his two grandsons.

While trolling the lake, hunting for the perfect place to cast their lines, Marlow noticed a man walking on water and felt it needed further investigating. As they approached, I collapsed against the strong winds and fell into the cold water.

"I'm sorry, I didn't mean to make you fall," Marlow called from his boat.

I struggled to pull my frigid body back on my board. "No, it wasn't you. This lake is giving me a beating."

Marlow offered to tow my paddleboard back to shore so I could live to fight another day. I accepted his offer, but I wasn't happy about it. I felt like I was reliving my first day of defeat all over again, but I dismissed the absurdity of such thoughts. It was a bad day on the water. Nothing more. I needed to find a way to accept that there would be more bad days in my future. Just because I was unable to log in an eighthour day of paddling, that didn't mean I was giving up. Marlow towed me back to the cabin where he and his grandsons were staying on the north side of the lake. Come to find out, I never entered Cass Lake. I was struggling in Alien's Bay the whole time. I called from a restaurant located at the campground and my dad arrived an hour later. We snapped a photo with Marlow and the boys, and I thanked them for the rescue.

The next day, Cass Lake was a mirror, smooth as silk, and I made it safely across in four easy hours. Proof in point:

what a difference a day can make.

One lake down. Big Winnie to go.

Lake Winnibigoshish is located in the Chippewa National Forest. This 67,000-acre behemoth is the fourth largest lake in Minnesota with over 140 miles of shoreline. Lake Winnie intimidated me. It was a menace at over fifteen miles at its widest point. Without help from river currents, it would take me an entire eight-hour day to navigate through the center, around the peninsula, and back into the Mississippi; most of which I would spend paddling alone, miles from shore.

My plan had always been to cross through the center. It would take a couple of days to hug the shore and I was feeling impatient. It was a risky decision. Boats have capsized due to large waves produced on windy days, and people have died. Strong winds can come out of nowhere, causing the lake to feel more like the ocean, and produce swells up to six feet. My map had a large caption printed on the lake that read:

Caution: High wind and waves may cause hazardous conditions. Paddling across the lake is not recommended.

Anglers that I met as I paddled down the Mississippi cautioned me to take the long route and follow the shoreline, but I was determined to go through the middle. Not because I wanted to disregard the warning, (I had learned that lesson on the river already), I just knew that I could do it, and on a hazy cool morning, I paddled off the dock at the Four Seasons Resort on the west side of Lake Winnibigoshish, and into the mist to prove my theory.

There was fear inside me towards Lake Winnie. I have no shame in admitting it. I imagined the lake to be the fresh water Bermuda Triangle, ready to devour me and transport me into another dimension once I reached the middle. Boats would pass by and see nothing but a paddleboard floating on the surface without a paddler. Headlines would read: *Lake Winnie Consumes Another Heedless Soul!*

A mile into my paddle, fog enveloped me—nothing but smoke on the water. I followed the faint light of the sun, but because of the fog, it was more of an ambiguous blotch than a definable sphere. Eventually, the pale yellow blotch disappeared. On such a big lake, no telling where I would end up in eight hours. I could very well spend the entire day paddling in circles and continue doing so well into the night.

From the map, I knew if I took a relatively straight course, following the sun, I would spot a peninsula jutting out to my right, and beyond that, my destination. If I could just catch a view of the other side. But without the sun, I had no idea where to point my SUP. After three hours of paddling blind, I began to feel a sense of panic. Perfect timing for my nemesis to arrive. It began with soft wisps against my cheeks, and then turned into quick gusts. If strong winds developed, not only would I be shrouded in gray, but I would also be fighting the waves to stay upright.

I decided it would be a good idea to take a lunch break and spend a few minutes in quiet meditation. My disorientation was getting the better of me. I'm a praying man. Whether or not something or someone is listening to me is not important. I'm a seeker, an explorer by nature, and I delight in the unknown. I sat on my board and munched on some trail mix. While floating gently through the mist, I said a prayer, something to the effect: "Hi, God. I realize your time would be best served if focused on a sick child, world hunger or a host of other things, but if you could be my compass for just a moment and help me find my way, I would sure appreciate it."

I finished and sat quietly eating my lunch. I remember U2's, *Beautiful Day*, was playing through my headphones, and before the song ended, sunlight blasted through the gloom and the fog began to burn away. I feared the coming winds, but those soft gusts were responsible for ushering out the fog and I soon found myself basking in light. I stood up and paddled towards the now definable sun and there, in the distance, was my peninsula. After another three hours, my dad's waving arms came into view.

Winnibigoshish was Winni-no-more.

In three weeks, I logged in over two hundred miles, and successfully crossed two of the biggest obstacles I would face in Minnesota. I could have left with my dad, holding my head up high, but we both knew that was not going to happen. I was going to hug him, tell him goodbye, and spend the next few months on the Mighty Mississippi alone.

Later that night, while searching for sleep, I reflected on my lessons from that first day on the river. No great thing is accomplished on our own. Even if perception dictates that we are alone, if we look back with honest eyes, we will probably find a generous spirit that helps along the way. My dad was there at every bridge and at the end of every day for three weeks. It deeply saddens me that people go through life without a father like mine. I have friends who belong to such a group, and I want to lend him out because we need someone on the bridge, cheering us on as we navigate the rivers in our lives.

No great thing is accomplished on our own.

Find what is good in your life and guard it with honor. There is no stopping the storms when they come. There is no avoiding failure and defeat when they find you unprepared, but like a lighthouse in the distance, there is good waiting for you. This, I promise.

ooo

My dad stayed on for another few days after Cass and Winnie, to see me through Grand Rapids and into Big Sandy Lake. He found a comfortable lodge on Lake Sandy to spend our last night together.

I think in some ways, being with me in the landscape of his childhood was healing for him. His parents divorced during his sophomore year in college. It was devastating to him and he never returned to Minnesota. Now, he had come back with his son. The son he witnessed bleeding out of his face just a short year ago, the son he believed would die in front of him in a hospital bed in Utah. His son was almost dead, but now he lives, and together, they were having a grand adventure.

When morning came and I awoke with a heavy heart. My dad was leaving, and the next twenty-two hundred miles were mine to face alone. In addition, the morning brought with it the revelation that I was no longer in second place. I was in third, made possible by the yellow SUP floating gently down river, two hundred yards in front of me.

My aspirations to become the first man to paddleboard the Mississippi were shared with two others: Alex Linnel from Minnesota and Dave Cornthwaite from merry old London, England. I first learned of them when I got off my plane in

Minneapolis. My dad stumbled across Alex's website while waiting for me to arrive and I found Dave's later that evening. It was a punch in the gut, but I felt I still had a chance. Alex had a seven-day head start but he was young and youth always falters when things get tough. Right? Never mind that he was built like a brick with a sixpack and I was, well... not.

Dave was ten days behind me. No way he would be a threat. After those first few weeks on the river, I began to accept the probability that I would lose the title of *Numero Uno* to Alex. My arrogance is bigger than my physical body wants to admit. However, I began to find acceptance in claiming the silver medal, but before I could find comfort in my second place status, I was demoted to bronze. I knew about Dave through his Facebook page. I could spot that bright yellow board anywhere. I had a two-week head start and now, I'd been lapped. I was the old man in third place, but I couldn't have given it up to a nicer bloke.

I came off the channel that connected the Mississippi to Big Sandy Lake, and that's when I spotted Mr. Cornthwaite. It took me about forty-five minutes to catch up to him and he was more than surprised to see me. Paddle boarding was a relatively new sport, though one that was catching on like sparks in a dry forest; however, seeing a paddleboard on the Mississippi River was a rarity. Dave figured out who I was right away.

From the moment I learned of my competitors, I developed characters in my head as to who my opponents would be. Would we cut off each other's heads with our paddles if we found ourselves on the river in the same stretch? Only one could be first. All others must be eliminated!

In my mind, Alex was the buff, young paddler who stole my dream of being the first with his abs and his Laird Hamilton signature paddleboard. But he couldn't steal something that was never mine in the first place.

Then there was a Mr. Dave Cornthwaite. He was the career adventure with all the gear, all the technology, and all the press. But in the flesh, he was just a nice guy with a vibrant smile. After an hour of paddling together, I felt even better giving up second place (not that I had a choice in the matter). Charismatic with a twinge of cheek, Dave is a cool cat, and I'm glad we got to meet. However, Dave was not slowing down for me, nor should he have. He picked up his personal pace, and I watched as he disappeared around the next bend. We are all on our individual journeys and should never judge another by their pace. Before Dave moved downriver, we made plans to meet at the same campground by sundown. It was great that I had a new friend to camp with that night, but all I could think about that day was my dad leaving. I love my dad very much, and the weeks shared together on the river made me appreciate him even more.

I reached the Palisades a couple of hours after Dave, and my dad offered to take us out for dinner before driving back to Minneapolis. It was a small little town, but we found a nice little restaurant with hot, home cooking. I prolonged the meal with chatter. I didn't want my dad to leave. It felt like a thirty-second meal, and before I knew it, he was paying the bill. We stood outside the café and I struggled for ways to grasp hold of the fleeting seconds. Dave clicked a photo of us, and then I hugged my dad. I think I hugged him as hard as he hugged me a year ago when I was dying in the hospital bed. I didn't shed tears, but not without effort. I watched him climb into the car and disappear from sight.

It was in the town of Palisade, Minnesota, where I said goodbye to my dad. He drove away and I felt the loneliness that I would experience for many days to come while paddling the Mighty.

Dave and I hit a little pub near the river for a beer and then returned to camp at the Berglund Park Campground. There wasn't much conversation that night. Dave had a routine to keep and would be up earlier than my body would allow. I left him to his blogging, thinking, "I should be blogging," but I was tired and sad. As I lay in my tent, trying to fall asleep, I started to feel a twinge of panic as the reality set in that I would be completely self-reliant in the morning.

When I awoke, Dave was gone, and I was alone for the first time since I started my journey.

FACEBOOK UPDATE
UNIVERSITY OF UTAH
MEDICAL CENTER.
JUNE 29, 2010

"Matthew, it's Dad, (his eyes half open) I love you, son." (he nods his head, yes.) A week ago today, I prayed as I drove like a crazy man from San Jose, Costa Rica, "God, please let him live until I hug him." That prayer was answered.

-Bill Crofton

6

The Incident

December 2009, **Playa** Flamingo, Costa Rica.
     I stood at the edge of the Pacific Ocean, bag of *Colones* (the local currency) in my hand, as the warm cobalt waters lapped my feet, causing them to sink into the black volcanic sand. The sun was warm, the day was beautiful, and I did not want to leave.

I was living the dream in Central America, working for a sailboat charter company. My dad and I run short-term Mission trips to the Guanacaste region in the Northern Pacific, and it had always been my goal to live there full time, so when the opportunity came for me to work for the charter, I left the States without so much as a glance over my shoulder. Four months later, they closed up shop. With no sailboat to sail customers into the sunset, there were no tips for Matthew to buy food. If you are a gringo who doesn't quite speak the language, it is nearly impossible to find work, so my only option was to come home and search for new beginnings.

The day before my departure, I went to a secluded beach just south of Playa Flamingo. The locals call it, *Bahia de los Piratas* (Pirate's Cove). There is a large rock about fifty yards off the coast with a cave midway up the face. Legend says that pirates would stash their treasures inside the cave before coming ashore.

I dropped my *Colones* into a leather drawstring sack, stuffed it in the leg pocket of my surf trunks, and dove into the warm, salty waters. I reached the rock, ascended the steep incline, and entered the dark mouth of the cave. I stepped into the steamy, bat-filled chamber and noticed that the floor was covered in blotchy white patterns. I walked towards the back right corner, knelt down and dug a small hole in the compacted soil. I dropped my bag of coins inside, grunted a raspy *"arrrgh"* and then covered it back up. It would be my "Matt was here" signature on the only country, besides the US, that I ever called home.

I was back in Florida just in time for Christmas, and by the end of January 2010, I had arranged a new adventure— from sailor to cowboy—as an employee for the R Lazy S Ranch in Jackson Hole, Wyoming. It was a family guest ranch, and I was to be a part of their maintenance team. The season ran six months, May thru October, and my employment included room and board, salary, and an end-of-season bonus. It was the first decent job I had landed after losing my construction business three years before in the dilapidated housing market. This would allow me to save for six months then use the money to travel and write the rest of the year before returning the following season.

I had an exciting year ahead of me, despite the lingering sadness that Costa Rica did not go as planned, but that's life and adaptation is key. There would be a few months to spend with family and friends before reporting to work in May; however, I used most of that time to begin my road to death.

The fevers began in March.

I don't remember the day, the hour or where I was. I just remember the pain. I would go from a balmy 98.6 degrees to 104 degrees in less than ten minutes. My body would shake uncontrollably and my teeth would clatter so violently that I feared they would break off in my mouth. I would surround my body with ice, wrapped in towels, and tremble for thirty-minutes before eventually drifting off to sleep. Every day was the same. They came on fast and brutal. When I felt them coming, there was deep anxiety that the next one would kill me. That's how painful they were. I endured the fevers for two weeks, thinking it was nothing more than a bizarre flu bug, before eventually giving in to a persistent mother who was pleading with me to get my blood tested.

It was the first step towards the most horrific experience of my life.

I will never forget the day I was admitted into Florida Hospital on April 15, 2010. My mom is the Director of Clinical Research for Florida Hospital Cancer Center. Because of her, I had the good fortune to be under the care of Dr. Lee Zehngebot. He had the suspicion, based on my symptoms and blood work, along with a CT-scan showing abnormalities in my liver, spleen, and lymphatic system, that Hodgkin's might be the culprit. I sat in his waiting room, holding my stomach, while he and my mom discussed my plight. Before they could finish, I stood up, ran to the bathroom, and started vomiting profusely. It felt as if my ribcage snapped apart and the jagged bones were piercing my skin. Dr. Z called for a wheelchair, and in less than an hour, I had an IV in my arm.

I spent two weeks lying in a hospital bed having my arms poked with needles five times a day with no result. I was expected to report for work in May, and the last thing I wanted was to lose my job at the R Lazy S Ranch. I needed answers.

On my tenth day as a guest at Florida Hospital, Dr. Zehngebot came into my room, frustrated with the lack of results and no longer convinced of his Hodgkin's theory. His thoughts were now leaning toward the idea that I was possibly having my first flare-up of an old malady.

In 2005, I was diagnosed with Sarcoidosis. There were no complications, so there wasn't a need for treatment. There was a lump on my forehead—that's how we caught it. Forgoing the idea that I was a man morphing into a unicorn, I decided to see a dermatologist. One biopsy later... Sarcoidosis. Dr. Z informed me that he was going to take a bone marrow sample and put me on Prednisone.

"Bone marrow. That's supposed to hurt like hell, isn't it?"

"You'll do fine."

I gripped the railing of my hospital bed as he forced the needle deep into my hip bone. Sure enough, the results came back: Sarcoid.

I was administered 20mg of prednisone and in less than twenty-four hours after my first dose, the fevers went away.

I had endured crippling fevers for over a month, and now they were gone.

By the time I was discharged and fully functioning again, the work season on the ranch had already begun, but they still wanted me to join the team. Their only requirement was that I bring a note from my doctor saying I was fit and healthy. I pleaded with Dr. Zehngebot to give me the green light. He obliged on the condition that I found a physician in Jackson Hole to monitor my steroid dose. After making promises to him and my family that I would stay on top of things, I hit the road once more.

Free Bird baby, I am indestructible.

Ten days later, the fevers returned.

I stayed on at the ranch from May to June and worked through the illness, doing my best to keep the severity to a minimum, and only reporting to my family with the basics. I'd wake up scalding, pack myself in ice until my temperature was down to at least a hundred degrees, and then stumbled out the door to work. I coughed like Doc Holliday and had a massive attack of strep throat. It was like swallowing razor blades every second of every day. When I went to the doctor in Jackson Hole, he suggested we shock the Sarcoid out of my system and increase the prednisone. Nothing helped, and I continued to get worse. I was ingesting 100mg of Prednisone a day and for anyone who's had experience with this particular steroid, you know that's a lot.

I managed to survive six weeks on that beautiful ranch with a view of the Grand Tetons outside my cabin. It was impossible to hide my illness from the crew, especially when I fainted in front of them while walking from one cabin to the next. Kelly Stern, owner of the ranch, was a Jackson Hole volunteer paramedic. There was no hiding anything from him. He could see the fever on my face every morning at breakfast. He'd tell me to go back to my cabin and lay down. He was such a kind soul and only wanted to help me but I felt guilty, lazy and weak. They were not getting their money's worth by keeping me on, so I decided the best thing would be to fly back to Orlando and readmit myself into Florida Hospital.

That night, I bought a ticket home for the following day, but never made it to the airport.

Morning came-a bright and beautiful blue morning in early June. I awoke and it felt like my guts were melting out of my bellybutton. I clutched my midsection and writhed in the sheets. I dug my fingernails so deep into my skin I caused it to bleed. Something was wrong, terminally wrong.

Brant, a fellow member of the maintenance crew, loaded me up in his truck and rushed me to the ER in Jackson Hole. It was the most agonizing twenty-minutes of my life. I felt as if I were dying; not the exaggerated phrase "I feel like I'm dying" but I physically felt my life was leaving me.

Brant helped me out of his truck, and I stumbled over to a trashcan and vomited, missing it by a foot. After an hour in the ER, the doctor came in and said I was too sick for their facility and that I would be airlifted from Jackson Hole to the University of Utah Medical Center. Nobody could tell me what was happening. I was a thousand miles away from my family, and feeling very frightened and alone.

They took me by ambulance to the airport and loaded me onto a medical airplane. I remember the pilot was wearing jeans. I thought that was cool. The male and female nurse team were so comforting as they went to work on my I.V.. The plane moaned to life, and I watched from my gurney through the porthole windows as the cotton-coated peaks of the Grand Tetons waved farewell against a curtain of clear blue sky.

After the plane landed in Salt Lake City, things began to get fuzzy. I remember bits and pieces. I was told later that my fading consciousness was attributed to a lack of oxygen in the brain, (but some would say I've always had a lack of oxygen to my brain).

My dad was running a mission trip in Costa Rica when my mom called him and said he needed to get to the hospital ASAP. I remember him coming into my room and hugging me. I remember my mom arriving. I remember craving a baked potato and a hamburger from Wendy's, and then I remember no more.

Several things happened after I slipped away. I lost sixteen days of conscious life and had to rely on my family to describe the events that pursued, which was difficult because what they faced during that time was nothing short of a parent's worst nightmare.

It can all be retraced back to the steps back to the cave in Costa Rica; the one with a carpet of bat crap. As it turns out, guano is highly toxic. It caused an infection in me called Histoplasmosis.

It's a common illness in different parts of the world. In the USA, it's abundant along the Ohio/Mississippi River valley throughout the farmlands. Birds poop in the soil and poor Farmer Brown breathes it in his lungs. In my case, bats pooped in the soil and poor wanna-be-pirate Matt breathed it in.

The acute form is practically harmless. The majority of those infected suffer from flu-like symptoms and it's easily treated. I wasn't one of the fortunate to contract the acute version. Mine was progressive disseminated. Left untreated, it has a fifty percent mortality rate. Coupled with an autoimmune disease and jacked up on extremely high doses of Prednisone, it was a death sentence. The doctors referred to it as the perfect storm and I had ridden the wave a lot longer than I should have.

They told my family if I made it through the night, it would be a miracle.

It was on a Wednesday, June 20, 2010, that I fell into a coma and was placed on life support. I endured multi-organ failure and massive internal bleeding. In addition, I suffered a reactive bone marrow infection (HLH) that caused my platelets to drop to below 5,000, (you're supposed to have over 150,000). My macrophages (specific white blood cells that ingest foreign material) were eating all the other cells in my blood. As fast as they would pump the blood in, my cells would devour it. I could no longer clot, and it poured from every hole in my face and pooled on the floor at my parents' feet.

This was over the course of twenty-four hours.

Day two of the coma, my little brothers Jonathan and Mark boarded a plane to say goodbye; at least that's how my parents prepped them. Jonathan and Mark got off the plane, came to the hospital, and walked into the room just as a minister was anointing my head with oil. It was to symbolize turning my body over to God to do what He will.

Some friends came to see me. There was a lot going on, and my parents advised them not to, but they didn't listen. Two of my best friends from grade school, Jason and Shawn, came to stand by my bed. My friend Johannie came up from Vegas and my friend Tara diverted her family's RV trip to Salt Lake just to come see me. Tara said she kissed my forehead. I never saw any of them. I don't remember a thing.

My body was so bloated with fluids and blood transfusions that I went from 190 lbs to 260 lbs. You couldn't tell where my thighs began and my ankles ended. The doctors worried that the skin on my shins would split open but the biggest fear, the one my mom states was her daily nightmare, was that I would throw a clot in my brain at any moment and that would be the end.

The edge. I was literally clinging to the edge every second of every day.

Two drugs treat Histoplasmosis. I was allergic to the first and it caused the skin to peel off my body. The second took hold and on July 4th, after sixteen days in a medically induced coma, I opened my eyes. Whether it was a coincidence that the Histoplasmosis I contracted from inhaling guano in Costa Rica came at the same time as my first symptoms or if it was the Histo itself that caused my Sarcoid to react we will never know... but the combination of both proved to be a deadly cocktail.

I woke up to find restraints around my wrists. They were to keep me from pulling the breathing tubes out of my mouth— not that I could because while in the coma my body devoured my muscle tissue. I couldn't move, except for my fingers. It was the most frightening, confusing experience of my life, to wake up choking, throat bulging and weeping phlegm, without the ability to move.

I was alive but in bad shape. My kidneys were so damaged that I was told I would be on dialysis for the rest of my life.

My liver was toast, and I was to be placed on an organ donor list. Every day was purgatory. I endured daily dialyses, daily transfusions, with little progress. Then, for reasons unclear to my medical team, two weeks after waking up, I peed for the first time. My kidneys began to function again. Shortly after, my liver began to regenerate. I still could not move, but I was slowly coming back from the edge. Once I could accomplish all the necessary steps to get me on a plane (getting into the wheelchair, then into the rental car, and on to the airport), I would be released to fly home where I would be readmitted to Florida Hospital.

It seemed like a relatively easy task to get into a wheelchair, but it wasn't, and I'll never forget the first time the physical therapist came into the room to stand me up. I lasted two seconds on my feet. It felt like I had 500lbs resting on my shoulders. Every day they would come and pull me out of bed. The PT assigned me exercises like trying to lift my heel an inch off the bed. It was a mental prison. My mind wanted something my body refused to do. It was so painful that sometimes I would pretend to be asleep when the PT came into my room. But I stayed with it and after six weeks at the University of Utah Medical Center, I boarded the plane for home. I sat next to my mother, doped up and drooling on her shoulder. She said it was one of the happiest days of her life.

I found out months later, while recovering at home, that my dad's prayers for me changed one morning while I lay in the coma. Hour after hour, he begged for the life of his son and then one day, he stopped begging and simply asked God's will on my life. He told me it was a turning point in a lifetime of faith and it begged the question, "Would I still believe if you took my son?" The following day, I turned my back on the abyss and started my journey towards recovery one creeping, crawling step at a time.

There are several examples of "coincidental intervening" from the day I left the ranch to when I was admitted into the ICU. I was never more than one miniscule decision away from death. I am traumatized to think of what the outcome could have been if someone had gone left instead of right. If I would have waited one more day on the ranch, they would have found a dead body lying in bed the next morning.

People sometimes ask me if I had a spiritual experience. I wish. I wish I could have seen the face of God or walked with Jesus. That would have been nice. Why didn't I see a white light like all the others? I've heard them on TV, talking about their near-death experiences. Mine was nowhere close. I was trapped and writhing, trying to draw breath. It was torture and the nightmares continue. I've tried to explain the place I was in a few times, but it's difficult. I will say this, and this will be all I say of it, when it was time for me to leave this world, a warm powerful presence fell upon me, and I was pulled back into the land of the living.

That's my testimony, for whatever it's worth. Maybe I just want to believe in something more... regardless if something more exists or not. Maybe I'm just a fool in love with mystery, unsettled by the fact that people are so certain in one thing or another. Maybe I'm just a fool.

My eyes opened but I could not focus. I was able to distinguish familiar voices, and I wanted to speak, but my mouth was full of plastic and the nurses were constantly having things sucked out so I wouldn't choke. How I longed to reach up and pull them out, but all I could do was lie there and feel the trickle of bloody tears roll down my cheeks.

People ask me what I remember most about that first day back from darkness. There are things I have pieced together with assistance, and there are things I remember in full focus.

I do remember her hands.

I could not open my eyes all the way, dried blood pasted them shut, but I would recognize my mother's hand by touch if you placed a hundred in mine. I remember they were always cold. They say death is cold. I believe my mom's hands were cold because she spent the last two weeks with them wrapped around death's throat, fighting for the life of her son. When she was in the room, she would hold my hand, and I never wanted her to let go. I would come in and out of consciousness, and her face was blurry. When she would get up to leave, I would try with all my strength to hold on, but my hands were bound. In a thousand years, I'll never understand what it was like for my mom to sit by and watch me die.

Another thing I remember was the singing.

My ears were crusted with old blood, like my eyes, but I would know his voice anywhere. It was my father. He would come into the ICU and sing "Jesus Loves Me" and place his hand on my forehead just as he had done every day during the coma. Whenever my dad placed his hand on my forehead and sang to me, he knew he might be saying goodbye. He was facing the test of, "Would I still believe in you if you take my son from me?"

I remember seeing the sunshine for the first time outside the hospital. I remember my friends, Shawn and David, waiting to greet me at the Orlando International Airport. I remember my last dialysis session and I remember what it was like to walk the first few steps without assistance. There is more to remember, but this was just a summary of the incident that occurred in the summer of 2010. Perhaps I'll write more about it someday.

I spent a total of two months in a hospital bed. First, in Utah under the care of Dr. Estelle Harris and her talented medical team (who I will forever acknowledge as the people who saved my life), and then back home in Orlando at Florida Hospital South under the care of my original care-givers, Dr. Lee Zehngebot and Dr. James McClelland.

My doctors in Utah told me to expect at least six months to pass before I could walk without some sort of assistance. I was off the walker in three and flying solo by four. They also told me to give it a year before making any rash life decisions, but I celebrated my year anniversary of being off life support paddleboarding the fourth largest river in the world.

I guess I've never been good at doing what I'm told.

I know there are things I will never forget. Perhaps I'll forever be haunted as the summer months approach with each new year. Probably not. Time has a way of taking care of such things. I will forever have both diseases inside me. The Histo lies dormant... waiting for a time where my immunity fails. I often endure pain from Sarcoidosis. Unfortunately, the steroids used to treat my Sarcoidosis is a catalyst for activating the Histo. Mother nature is a mad scientist. When the sarcoid symptoms are too much to endure, I opt for taking Prednisone but have to be monitored daily for any sign of Batman's return. The horrors I endured led to a mighty journey, so I will not complain. It has been a most excellent adventure.

I can say, however, greatly earnest: No matter where life takes me beyond the river... for the rest of my days... I'm staying the hell way from bats.

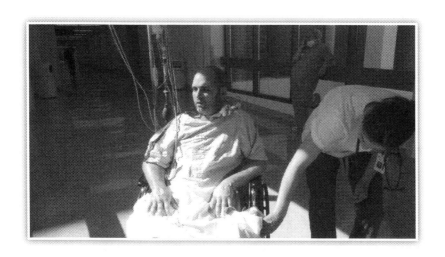

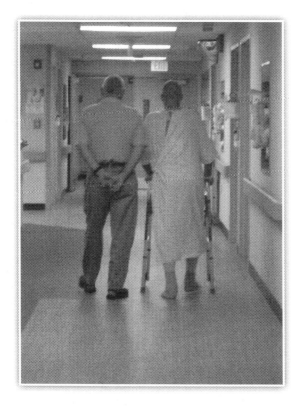

RIVER JOURNAL,
JUNE 23, 2011.

Thank you, Tom and Charlotte
Chatfield, for the wonderful
company, a cozy bed, and
scrumptious breakfast burritos!
My friendship cup runneth
over. Randomly meeting
you kayaking with your
family turned out to be a true
Mississippi River oasis! Perhaps
you'll open your door to more
weary travelers who don't give
off a "creep vibe."

7

The Bridge

Morning came and I felt odd and isolated. Dave had already broken camp and was well on his way to Aitkin. We made plans the night before to camp another night together, but he would reach our destination hours before I would.

It was a sad day on the river for me. Seeing my dad at every overpass had been encouraging. It helped to relieve the badgering thoughts that for every slow mile I paddled, there were thousands more to go. With one fatherless bridge after another, I sank deeper into loneliness.

I reached Aitkin just before the sun fell beyond the tree line, and while I was setting up camp, a couple were pulling their boat from the water. They saw my paddleboard and asked what I was doing. I told them I was paddling to the Gulf, and then I asked them if they could point me in the direction of the nearest grocery store.

They didn't point. They drove me to the store and then on a hunt to find WiFi so I could catch up on my blog. They gave me their cell number and told me when I was finished, they would come pick me up and bring me back to the campground. The next morning, I awoke to find a grocery bag with bread and blueberries sitting outside my tent and I had my suspicions as to who placed them there. I would soon learn that without this kind of outpouring of generosity on the river, I would not get far. My third night on my own, I slept under a bridge in the town of Crosby. As I shivered in darkness, I thought to myself, "Please don't let this be the adventure that awaits me downriver."

As the day melted into dusk, I was still a few miles from Crosby. Clouds swelled black and bled rain. With visibility compromised, I had suspicions that I passed my campsite. My DNR maps were conveniently marked with places to camp. Wooden signs with an inverted "V" resembling a tent crudely etched into them were used to mark the actual campsites in the field. They were no bigger than a license plate and blended in nicely with tree bark. Some campgrounds were easy to find, while others were tucked into the woods and good luck to you.

Whether I missed it or not, thanks to the darkness and rain, the bridge would be my home for the evening. I didn't set up a tent. I just rolled out my sleeping bag, got naked, and climbed in. I have to admit, it was cozy. The rain methodically pitter-pattered as I stretched inside my soft sleep sack, allowing my muscles to sigh in relief. A few hours passed and the rain softened. Sleep eluded me, so I climbed the bridge to the road and there it was, through the fog, a brightly lit mirage in the distance. It was a sports bar called The Bridge. Perfect, I'm sleeping under a bridge and eating at The Bridge. I remember on my motorcycle road trip back in 2008, sitting in a pub and having a Sam Adams Boston Lager while looking at Sam Adams' grave. Obviously, I'm easily entertained.

Until that night, my focus was solely on the day's paddle, and then I would spend the evenings with my dad. The Bridge was my chance to make new acquaintances and tell my story. I knew the impact it could make. While in the hospital, my dad would post updates on Facebook each morning. It didn't take long for the news to reach far beyond friends and family. Thousands were glued to his posts each day, waiting for the slightest hint that life was returning to me. Those same people were watching me now as I grappled with the river. It humbled me to know that so many would root for such a nobody.

My warm-up on the river was over. It was time. The calling, the true heartbeat of this journey was to share my story. I entered The Bridge, sat at the bar and ordered the biggest burger on the menu. It wasn't long before I made eye contact with Ryan and gave my usual, "How's your night going?"

Within minutes, I was surrounded. By the time I finished my cheeseburger and reports of miracles, Jo, the owner, handed me fifty dollars, Shane gave me ten, and my new friend Ryan gave me twenty dollars! I put up a fight. I didn't want this to become a habit that when I told my story, people stuffed cash in my hands. But these Midwesterners got angry when I refused. I asked them to donate that money to the charity on my website; they said they would, but they weren't letting me leave without the money they offered. After some laughs with my new friends, I walked back to my campsite and muscled a few hours of sleep before moving on in the early a.m. I'm sure if I had told them I was sleeping under a bridge, they would have done something about it, but they already gave me hard-earned money out of their own pockets, and that was all the help I would allow that evening. I told my story and it made somebody feel good. It was a good start... a new start... and a new start is what I needed the most.

The months before my journey down the Mississippi River, I was losing myself to depression. The days following my coma, I experienced a euphoric high. I was so happy to be alive and I was thankful for every moment. After spending two months in the hospital, I returned home in July of 2010, and spent the next four months learning how to walk again. I gave it all I had; every ounce of hope and determination I could muster. And then, I simply had no more.

Soon after, the darkness fell upon me, and then came the nightmares.

It started in December of 2010 and lasted until I bought my plane ticket to Minnesota in May 2011. I'd lie in bed all night staring into nothingness, pretending to watch television, waiting for that magical twilight hour where I would find sleep. Then came the dawn with its awful sunlight poking through small cracks in the window blinds, stabbing at my eyeballs with tiny shimmering daggers. My eyes would hurt so bad it made me angry. I'd roll out of bed and punch the defiant louver responsible for allowing dawn to thrash me out of slumber, but three more would flop open from the impact, resulting in a flood of angry sunlight causing me to recoil like a vampire, spitting and cursing.

When I was awake, sadness was the first sensation that ushered me into another day. Sadness followed by immediate hopelessness. My stomach felt like it was marinated in battery acid all night—boiling and gurgling—and it hurt just to be alive.

It was a sad story. I went from physically dying in a hospital bed to wasting away emotionally back home. Daylight hours fell away while I slept; people lived, the world turned, and I'd wake just in time to hate myself for missing life for another day. But then it was happy hour. I'd throw on jeans and head to the bar. "Probably shouldn't be drinking," I'd tell myself, due to the fact that I was on daily dialysis just a few months ago. But that was then, and this is now and a pitcher of beer was only five bucks at the pub near my house.

How should I have been living? When overwhelming odds point to death and then there is a miraculous recovery, how should a person celebrate that second chance at life? With feelings of unbridled happiness and thanksgiving, I thought. When I walked the line between life and death, I swore, if given the chance, I would make each day count with passion and purpose. So much for empty promises!

I cut through the woods and crossed the golf course, taking time to shuffle through the sand trap because that's what an asshole does. I'd walk, head down, hands in pockets, and obsess over why I felt the way I did. I'd think about all those survival stories on TV. I hated them because the victims were just *so* damn happy just to be alive. You could hear it in their voice, the eternal gratitude they had for every day; it was smeared across their pious, little faces. I felt none of those things. In fact, I wished I could have passed my life on to someone who would soar higher than I ever could. I wanted to give my life to a poor kid with a terminal illness. Why spare my life over an innocent child's? I was asleep. The coma came so fast, there was no time for fear, and if death had claimed me, I would have been none the wiser.

Why's are worthless. I did wake up, but to nothing more than a scrap of who I used to be, and now, I was drowning in emotional abyss. I'd stay awake all night in fear and sleep all day in denial. I checked out and no longer had a passion for life. I was scared all the time, scared of death, and the nightmares never stopped.

I'd slip unnoticed through the entrance of my favorite sports bar and claim my usual rickety oak stool, isolated in the darkest corner of the room. I kept my head down and scribbled on napkins but inevitably, as the night wore on, curiosity got the better of them, and someone always came looking for a story. I couldn't blame them. That's how I used to be. It was my favorite part of being on the road. I lived for the sharing of stories, the sharing of life. It always amazed me how I could roll into Anytown, USA, and find the same desires throughout the country.

We are so lonely. Research indicates that people listen for seventeen seconds before interrupting. I honed my skills during my excessive wandering, making sure to look people in the eye and pause before I spoke. I can paint pictures of glorious landscapes, cobalt skies and the poetic winding roads that I consumed on two wheels, but it's the people I remember the most.

But I'd suppress my desire to share because, in my current state, I didn't want to talk or listen. I just wanted them to leave me alone. However, sometimes, if the planets aligned at the precise moment and the right person asked with obvious sincerity, I would cave—most likely from loneliness— and tell them of my malady.

Whether it was a male or female I was addressing, I could usually expect different reactions. It would start with unintentional eye contact or someone would simply be curious about the words I was writing on those tiny, snow white napkins. If the inquiring party was a dude, their reactions were a slack jaw and a furrowing brow, followed by a, "Holy shit, man."

If I were speaking to a woman, and she had kids of her own, inevitably, as the story unfolded, motherly instincts would kick in as she imagined her own children with tubes protruding from their mouths and blood pouring from their eyes and ears. The tears fell and I felt guilty for bringing sadness to their otherwise peaceful evening. I apologized for telling them about it, hinting that next time I'd keep it to myself. That's when the reactions, both male and female, would become desperate, almost intrusive, as they grabbed me firmly by both arms and tried reasoning with me in a genuine, momentary sobriety. "You must share your story." It made me feel timid and I didn't like the attention.

Surrounding patrons who listened in, though never spoke, concurred with the plea with quivering lips and glistening eyes.

Subjects like God and miracles soon followed, but I shrugged them off before my own tears began to fall. I gave props to modern medicine even though I knew the truth. I was there and I heard what the doctors said. There was a point in time where medicine had nothing to do with it, but I hate when people try to force experiences and beliefs on others for which there is no proof. I shared with them my philosophy that no matter what you believe, you should care more about living it than proving it. The more minutes that pass, the less any of it makes any sense. Last call would come and we'd end our brief connection with sloppy hugs and slurred goodbyes and promises that I would live the miracle of my experience.

Once a week, I managed to enter the world of day-walkers and visit my counselor. The doctors told me that I might experience things, unhappy things, in the months to come. I'd sit in my chair and cry of days past and present—who I used to be, who I was supposed to be—and how "the incident" had changed my life forever. One afternoon, I remember telling her that my birthday was coming up, and if I didn't do something... now... I would load my .38 and make it my last.

It wasn't just Costa Rica and the events that followed. That was simply the deadly frosting on a sad cake. I spent my twenties failing miserably at a number of pursuits, personal and professional. But in my thirties, when everything I worked for was taken away, I began living for the first time. I found a passion for writing, and I lived on the road, flowing from town to town, gathering stories. I knew what I wanted to do with the rest of my life and there was a sweet freedom in that.

I was thirty-three when I took my first great adventure. All I had left from my former life were a few packed boxes, a backpack, a sleeping bag and a beautiful black and chrome Honda Shadow. I spent a year biking 30,000 plus miles through forty-four states, sleeping under bridges and in the company of friends and strangers, forging some of the greatest memories of my life. After the motorcycle, I did some hitchhiking out west, lived in Costa Rica, and then wound up working on a ranch outside of Jackson Hole, Wyoming, that bordered the most majestic mountains in America. The Grand Tetons. It was there that the illness began.

I would think about those memories and the life I was creating while watching Family Guy at 3 a.m. in a drunken stupor. I allowed pain to be an excuse. Living in constant pain is tough on your mental health. I missed the physical strength I had before the incident. I was never a gym guy and my strength was not a product of lifting weights. I was carpenter strong. My strength came from carrying three sheets of plywood at a time. I was surfer strong. My strength came from paddling the ocean, accumulating hundreds of miles over a lifetime. My dad would hug me and say, "My son is like a brick!" But after the hospital, I would look in the mirror and all I saw was a sagging chest and bones protruding from my back. I looked pale and my bright blue eyes were hollow and pitted. I never understood brokenness until those days.

Word spread quickly when I was in the coma. I opened my eyes after two weeks and learned that thousands, spanning oceans, were praying for my family and my recovery. I had a Facebook page created in my honor by my best friend's wife, Rachel. She titled it *"Get Well Soon, Prayers for Matt."* Every morning, sitting at a table in the Starbucks located on the first floor of the University of Utah Medical Center, my dad would post updates on my page while my mom stood devoted to my bedside in the I.C.U. After my awakening, my knowledge of the events that almost claimed my life were still a mystery to me, but apparently the incident was so unique and disturbing that the story grew wings and took flight. People who didn't believe in God or hadn't for some time, wrote and told me that because of my struggle, they were praying again. They were hugging their children longer, loving their husbands more deeply or adoring their wives more intensely.

I was taken off life support on the fourth of July. The following day, my mother placed a laptop on my bloated stomach and opened the Facebook page that Rachel had created for me, so that I could scroll down through sixteen days of family, friends, and people unknown to me, begging God for my life. The tears welled up and pushed through dried blood and crust before falling down my face. I watched videos of children singing songs to me and clicked through posted pictures of my life from high school and beyond. If I ever wanted to know what my funeral would be like, I could now see it across the computer screen. It was the most humbling experience of my life: To be loved so dearly and to see it proclaimed so extravagantly.

Something had to change. I wanted to make them proud. I wanted to feel proud, for me, before my pride walked away and I lost it forever. I began to plot and scheme as to how I could jumpstart my life once more. I was alive... and I had a paddleboard. With those humble offerings, a mighty journey was born.

A year later, there I was, sleeping under a bridge by the Mississippi River in northern Minnesota. It wasn't pleasant, but instead of staggering out of the bar drunk, I'd brought some hope to people I'd never met. Maybe it was the beginning of healing for me, but who knows such things. I still had long way to go, and the reality of my river adventure was quickly embedding as I spent many a night alone after the bridge. Days on the river can seem like weeks. The current was not as fast as I anticipated, and I would drag through each day, mostly because my board was still carrying too much weight. Old Blue was not the equipment best suited for such an endeavor, but he kept me dry for the most part. The river flowed and the hours melted into one another.

I complained a lot about the winding Mississippi in Northern Minnesota. Sometimes it would bend so sharply that it would turn back on itself. I'd actually lose the yards I just paddled, or so it felt that way. All day long, large deer fly would bite and bounce off my head while swarms of mosquitoes threatened to carry me back to Florida. However, looking back, this stretch of the Mississippi was by far the rawest and most beautiful that it would ever be. There were clear, cool waters, quaint river towns and enormously generous, beautiful people.

I believe Earnest Hemmingway said it best: "The world is a beautiful place and worth fighting for."

Northern Minnesota.

People of the river. The heart of adventure.

Breakfast!

Last day with my dad.

RIVER JOURNAL,
JULY 2, 2011

Most stories go unnoticed as we
pass each other on the streets. Most
miracles go unseen. The people that
hurt us sleep easy, and the people
that love us lead a life of their
own. at the end of the day, while
lying in the dark staring at the
ceiling, the responsibility is ours to
be satisfied with the result of who
we are... and the direction we are
paddling.

8

Inventing the Apperts

I sprang from sleep in a panic, scraping my head against the slick orange ceiling of my tent. More nightmares again, coma nightmares, involving bleeding faces and other horrible things.

"Where am I?"

Sweat dripped from my forehead as I acclimated to my surroundings. I could always tell when I had overslept on the river because after 7 a.m., the sun turns my tent into an oven. I sat in my fabric crockpot trying to choke my anxiety.

"I'm not dying. I am *not* dying."

The static heat helped to motivate me out of my tent and into a new day. I crawled from the opening, still disoriented. A soft breeze came off the river and cooled my face. The fresh air was calming. I closed my eyes and welcomed the reassurance: "I'm not at home, in a fetal position, chained to my depression. I'm on the river. I am free."

I was, however, alone in my tent on the Fourth of July.

Waves of sadness and isolation began to gently lap against my heart, but I did my best to force them back. This was a day to celebrate. I've always loved the Fourth of July, but this was one to remember. I was desolate spending it absent of family and friends. No telling where I would be on the river, but wherever I ended up, there had to be a party. This entire expedition was centered on a celebration of life. A celebration of *my* life. For last year, I declared independence from my ventilator.

My actual awakening was on July 2, but it was two more days before they could remove those satanic plastic tubes from my throat. I may not remember my first breath at birth, but I'll never forget the first breath of my second birth as the tubes slid out and I coughed and spit my lungs back to life.

It was indeed a day for celebration. However, as the morning moved into noon, I had yet to see another soul on the river, and an internal fog began to move through me. I fought it all morning, making promises that I would be happy, but I was feeling so alone. Subconsciously, the memories of last year where condemning me into another round of depression and I needed help. I needed a family.

By mid-afternoon, I landed in Brainerd and was offered a warm bed, thanks to some generous people I met as I approached the north end of town. Debbie was kayaking with her son when I paddled by. Curiosity was piqued and they asked what I was riding. I shared my story and Debbie invited me to stay at her parents' cabin on the river.

I was thankful that I would have some company on the fourth, but their plans took them elsewhere, and I ended up wandering aimlessly for the rest of the day. I followed unfamiliar streets through an unfamiliar town and stumbled upon a little pub called *Yesterday's Gone*—appropriate name for a man such as me—located uniquely under a water tower, and moved my solitary celebration indoors. The bartender who kept me company that night gave me a free beer after some small talk that eventually led to why I was in town and my reasons behind paddling the Mississippi River. Little did he know, he was my family on that celebratory day of life. Our conversation was light and I preferred it that way. I finished my beer, we shook hands and I continued exploring the town.

I did everything I could to make my year anniversary off life support something to remember, but without loved ones to share in significant milestones, they simply passed by in melancholy silence. I think this set me up for additional gloomy days over the next week as I paddled downstream through quaint river towns, absent of thought; like a piece of driftwood.

ooo

Almost a month on the Mississippi and Minneapolis continued to elude me. As far as I was concerned, I would remain on the river, in this state (state of mind, state of geography, doesn't matter) forever. I kept busy paddling and sharing my story of death and resurrection with the people of the river, but every night I found myself feeling very much alone. That's when I made up my imaginary family.

As I floated down the same old straits and rounded the same old bends, I would daydream that my pretend family was waiting for me around the next curve. There, I would find an exquisite riverfront home fully equipped with a happy family with arms wide open. Turn after turn, but they did not come. Night after night I spent on the cold hard ground, eating canned ravioli, and then up again the next day.

Repetition. Brutal repetition.

My disease was on the attack, and my joints cried out with every mile I paddled. I severely underestimated my condition. I was still a very sick man though I would never admit it. I was weak, weary, and heavy laden. If something didn't happen soon, some sort of outstretched hand to bring me encouragement that what I was doing had meaning, I would soon paddle to shore, leave Old Blue, and head on home.

And then, one day, they were there.

It was my longest day on the river so far. I beat my personal best by completing thirty-two miles. My drinking water was gone and the sun had baked me to a nice golden crisp. As I entered the town of St. Cloud, I noticed a familiar sign on the left side riverbank hanging above a dockside Tiki Bar. It was a yellow surfboard with a shark bite taken out of it and big letters across the face that spelled, "Landshark."

Landshark is Jimmy Buffet's beer, brewed in Jacksonville, Florida. I'd recognize that sign anywhere. I don't know why I paddled close to it; maybe I wanted to be near something familiar. My intentions were to paddle right on past, but then I heard a voice.

"Where are you going?" Collette Appert called from the dock.

"The Gulf of Mexico! Am I close?"

Chris Appert, Collette's husband, jumped to his feet.

"Do you need anything? Some water?" "Water would be amazing," I answered.

The Apperts were having a relaxing afternoon by the river with their kids and a few friends when they fished me from the water. Chris stuck a cold beverage in the palm of my hand, and my story quickly followed. I had their full attention. I spoke of blood and brokenness and Collette's motherly instincts began to surface on her face. I could tell she was imagining herself in place of my mom, wondering what it would be like to see her own children in such a horrid condition. So, sheepishly, I moved on to happy river talk.

After a peaceful hour, laughing and sharing, they with their hospitality and I with my stories, the Apperts invited me to stay and have dinner. It was pot roast night. You can imagine my excitement hearing those words after many nights of solitude, sleeping in a tent on a hard dirt floor, and eating cold ravioli out of a can. And it only gets better. Chris informed me that I would be sleeping in their guesthouse. No tent for me tonight. I'm not sure what he saw in this grubby river rat that made him feel comfortable enough to invite a stranger into his home, but I'd like to think it was something similar to how I felt about him. I felt as if he had been a lifelong friend, and Collette, the sister I never had. It could have been my imagination, or it could have been river fever, but the Apperts felt like home, and I already cared for them like family.

Their two teenage girls, Raven and Madison, picked me up in a golf cart and chauffeured me over to the guesthouse. When Collette opened the door and welcomed me in, I almost released my bladder on the warm wood floors. I'd never seen such a place. It was like living in the trees because all I could see through the wall of windows were swaying green branches and the gentle waters of the river. She took me on a tour of the apartment and showed me its many lavish amenities, but my attention was divided between two primary indulgences: the promise of a steamy beef feast and the giant bed that I would be sleeping in that night. It had one of those memory foam mattresses and it would soon have the imprint of a very happy paddler.

Meat and potatoes came in abundance with the Apperts. If I were from the North, I probably would have recognized the name. Turns out, Chris Appert is one of the largest food distributers in the northwest; hence, the amazing property on the river, but I would have never guessed it. Chris and Collette were some of the most humble, gracious people I have ever had the privilege to share company with, and their children were a pleasure as well.

You see, adventures for me are more about the people I encounter and the stories shared than the solitude of nature or pushing my limits. They all have their place and I enjoy them all, but I'm a writer first, and as a writer, I feed off the random encounter, and sometimes these encounters prove to be more rewarding than I ever could have imagined. Maybe it was the timing. Maybe it was simply that I needed them at that moment, or maybe it was something more... something special. I think they felt the same; otherwise, I wouldn't have spent the next two days living with the Apperts. It wasn't the comforts they provided me, although luxurious and extremely appreciated. I would have slept in my tent just to hang out with them a little more. I was a part of a family again, if only for a moment. Chris, Collette and their children, Mason, Raven, and Madison, felt like "home away from home" for me.

The next day we took their pontoon boat out to the sandbar, and I got to experience the river in a different way, not as a force of nature to conquer, but as a family chilling in the cool waters; just good food, good company. I tried to get the kids on the paddleboard, but Mason was the only Appert who dared. "Maybe next time, girls!"

When I left their company two days later to return to the Mighty, Chris and Collette stocked me with food and water; then they hugged me in a way that caused me to shed tears a mile downriver. They gave me what I needed when I needed it most: a family, and a healthy dose of courage to continue with my journey.

RIVER JOURNAL,
JULY 9, 2011

Tyler and Cheryl! How are you
my dear friends? i received your
donation and i cannot thank
you enough! you showered me
with kindness while i was on
my motorcycle-Tyler said it was
"donating to the arts." i still laugh
about that-and it appears that your
kindness towards me has no end. i
love you, my friends! until we meet
again-keep the fireplace empty and
at room temperature!

"Kindness is a language which the deaf can hear
and the blind can see."

—Mark Twain

9

The River Jordan

Lock and Dam 1 loomed in the distance, flanked by the Twin Cities.

It felt like only a moment had passed since my dad and I loaded the van and set out for the headwaters. His return trip took less than three hours; mine over thirty days. It's safe to say, reaching Minneapolis took a bit longer than anticipated. She was a lovely sight nonetheless, postured against a pale blue sky.

There still lingered a naivety in me that believed I could catch up to my competitors, but it didn't come around as much anymore. The Matt that paddled most days was the guy having too much fun learning and laughing with the people of the river. Today, however, was about business. I was about to be schooled by the Army Corps of Engineers and the infamous Mississippi River lock systems.

The only thing I knew about locks was from a special on the Discovery Channel about the Panama Canal. A dam separates the difference in the river's elevation. It spans across the entire river, and on one side, there is a long concrete chamber with iron gates on both ends called a lock. A lock is a device for raising and lowering boats and barges between stretches of water of different levels. Boats pull into one end of the lock and the door closes. Water is then pumped out to the appropriate level and the chamber opens on the opposite end. Level heights can vary from a few feet to more than forty feet.

I knew I had to face twenty-nine locks on the Mississippi River. Today would be my first and I'd be lying if I said I wasn't intimidated. People along my path kept warning me that the lock operators would not let me through; I would have to get out and portage around, but I was going to give entering the lock a shot. The mist rose and Anthony Falls roared against the Minneapolis skyline. My adrenaline was pumping as I hugged the west shore to avoid the 55' drop. The lock was empty, so I paddled up to the entrance and pulled the cord. The alarm buzzed and Jodie, the lock operator, spoke to me over the loud speaker and asked me to wait five minutes. The red stoplight flashed green and I paddled through amongst the funky smells of dead fish and debris.

Jodi peered over the rail where I stood ten feet below. "What is that and what in the hell are you doing?"

I smiled, "It's a stand-up paddleboard. I'm taking it to the Gulf."

"Wow, you are either extremely courageous or a few cards shy of a full deck."

"I'd put your money on the latter," I said.

Jodie showed me where to hang on and informed me that the lock would close and the water level would drop 55'. She wished me luck, snapped a picture on her phone, and went back to the station. I held on and giggled as the massive iron doors clanked shut and the water began to drop. I watched the railing as it moved from ten feet above my head to more than fifty. I took a cool picture of the tip of my board with the mighty gates consuming the foreground. Thirty minutes later, the gate swung open and Minneapolis lay before me. I waved goodbye to Jodi and hello to the Twin Cities. It was a scene as I paddled south. People in buildings waved and commuters stood by the river pointing in disbelief.

After thirty-eight miles, one of my longest days so far, I came around a bend below the twin cities and heard someone calling me from the outside deck of a restaurant. It was the Pool and Yacht club, the only exclusive club on the Mississippi River. Chris Nichols was intrigued to see a river rat on a large surfboard floating by and wanted to buy me a drink, so I beached my SUP and dragged my gear up on the muddy bank.

I must have been quite a sight when I entered the restaurant with my soggy backpack, squishy flip-flops and the stink of dead fish. I weaved through the cloth-covered tables amongst the classy patrons, towards the outside deck where Chris sat with his friends. I sat down in all my grimy glory; scruffy bearded and reeking. Chris bought me a cold beer in a fancy glass and we all sat watching the river boats float by and spoke of my adventure. Before I left, the owner of the Yacht Club gave me a flag with the company name on it. I told her it would wave proudly alongside my American flag and pirate flag all the way down the river. I was later featured in their local newsprint, the *Scuttlebutt*.

I floated away from Chris and company into a quiet few days of solitude. I was determined to close the Minnesota chapter before my first month was over, but it took just shy of six weeks. Each morning, I made lofty goals to paddle somewhere between forty or fifty miles, but at the end of the day, I would never average more than twenty-five. My broken body cared little for my daily goals. My competitors paddled at least fifty-plus miles a day, every day. It was safe to say, slow and steady will not win this race. But I was loving everything about the river. The growing pains were evident those first few weeks after my launch, but after a month, I had become part of the river. Everything found purpose in its flow. Good days, bad days; they were all simply "river days". Each moment flowed gently into the next, and within every moment, there was something to feel good about. My campsites were becoming increasingly unique as I drifted further south. I became a master of concealed residences. I could sniff out cozy out of the way spots, within walking distance to town, where I would stock up on noodles and water. Sometimes, I would sneak into backyards at night and use a garden hose to shower before heading back to camp, unnoticed, where I could read and rest in my canvas of solitude. I envisioned before taking my Huckleberry adventure that every night there would be a campfire and a warm meal. In reality, if someone did not pass by on a boat and hand me some food or invite me to dinner, I ended up having a cold can of noodles. I found more joy in reading books, exploring and meeting people than I did in taking time to prepare meals.

Routine set in, and my life on the river was simply my life on the river. There were days of laughter and friendship and then days of silence and loneliness, and I cherished them both. As I closed another long day, I saw some guys swinging like monkeys from a rope swing and drinking homemade moonshine out of a cork top jug and thought: "Yep, I'm camping here."

"Dude! What are you doing?" One called from the river's edge. "Paddling to the Gulf of Mexico!" "What! No way!" He laughed.

I ran the end of my SUP onto the muddy bank, and made introductions with Ben. He handed me the rope (have to initiate before hanging with this river brood). I took my turn on the swing, smashed my toe, and then took a swig of homemade moonshine. "Damn!" I choked, eyes snap-popping like a shiny pinwheel.

I really felt like a character out of a Mark Twain novel hanging with the boys, whooping and hollering like apes on a vine. Ben invited me to hang out with him and his friends for the evening. They waited while I set up camp near the rope swing. Then, I followed them into the little town of Clearwater, where they led me to a hot meal and some cold beer.

This is what I do on the river when I do not wish for solitude. I meet people and practice the art of listening, which is very difficult thing to do. Whenever I catch myself formulating my own sentences in my head, waiting for my turn to speak, I mentally slap myself. It is difficult because people instantly want to know what I'm doing and want to hear about it. However, I look for openings to divert the subject and ask about their lives, but when they get me on the coma stuff, there's no turning back no matter how hard I try and change the subject.

My friends back home would tease me about the river pictures I posted, accusing me of too much partying and not enough paddling. They are probably right, for it was a party to be alive. I thrive on this way of life. It's my addiction to enter a town I've never been and see people I've never met and win friendships. It's like finding treasure strewn about the banks of the Mississippi. People rub shoulders every day, yet we feel so isolated. I never truly understood the power of listening. It can change lives, you know. People want to tell their stories and I want to hear them. Perhaps this is not a memoir of me on the river but a "them-oir." And you can't spell them without a backwards me. That could be the moonshine typing.

Throughout the night, between roars of laughter and palms slapping tables, Ben would pull me aside and tell me how he wanted to drop everything and do what I was doing. "Come on!" I'd tell him. He'd get a puzzled look like he was thinking on it and I knew that look well. I learned to banish that look from my own face. It meant I was over-thinking and would never do anything.

"Don't think, just do!" I yelled above the noise in the lively pub. "Yes, it can get you in trouble sometimes, but it's a hell of a ride!"

The bar closed and I strolled down the dark street, with my new pals, towards camp. I told Ben before we parted ways that I wanted to spice things up a bit. I needed to break the daily routine and he informed me that I was just in time for Riverfest in Monticello, a town just a few miles south (a day's paddle on the river, of course).

It was a big deal, an annual festival spanning four days. On the last day, they would drop a thousand ducks from the bridge crossing the Mississippi River for the big Duck Race. I wanted to be in the water the moment the town tossed the quackers from the bridge and I really wanted to be wearing a duck costume when they did it. Unfortunately, my dreams splattered on the muddy banks when I learned they were rubber (it kind of lost its appeal after that, but better for the ducks). No matter, it was something different and I was all about it.

The last thing I anticipated was to experience something in Monticello that would forever change the emotional and spiritual course of my river expedition.

ooo

The following morning, I left Clearwater and paddled hard for Monticello. Minnesota was holding me tight and I wondered if I would ever make it to Iowa. Did Iowa even exist or did Minnesota stretch all the way to the Gulf of Mexico?

I was floating in a steaming hotpot of "Matt" all day and I just wanted to set up camp and hunt down a soda (I craved ice-cold fountain drinks ferociously on the river). I paddled under the famous bridge where the ducks would fall, and stopped at a boat ramp on the edge of Monticello around 3 p.m. The riverside park was being used to set up the arts and crafts segment of the festival, but I missed it by an hour. Several local venders straggled behind, taking down booths, packing up campers, so they could be in town for the big concert. I approached a group of people standing next to a Henna artist to inquire about camping, but as I ventured closer to the pack, they paid little attention to me. Most people look upon me with curiosity: this soggy, sun-stained flotsam floating about on an obscure piece of foam. The distraction was obvious when I noticed the puppy sleeping at their feet. I would be more interested in a puppy, too.

There were maybe five or six people gathered around, but I noticed Jordan right away. She was with her mother, Tara, and her five-year-old sister, Jillian. She stood proudly displaying her surgical scars across the top of her chest and had nothing to hide her thinning hair. Her smile was like a ray of sunlight breaking through gurgling storm clouds. Her bright eyes showed no sign of struggle, but on the inside, I could only imagine what kind of wars raged. I could tell she was sick, but not because she acted the part. She displayed such a powerful calm. Perhaps the two words fail to complement each other, but if you were there, you would know what I mean.

I introduced myself to the group and asked about camping in the public park. They were unsure, but after we exchanged some small talk about why I was paddling the river, Tara graced me with an invitation to set up camp at their house. Tara had some reservations about a strange man in her backyard, as any mother would have. I think an axe was mentioned, like, she would put the axe to me if I turned out to be a psycho, but in the end, she told me if her husband was comfortable with it, then I was welcome to stay. I knew he would be because I'm a nice guy. That's not arrogance talking; that's a hundred people on the Mississippi River all making the same claim that I don't give off a "creep vibe."

Life is simple on the river. Two questions linger at day's end: Where do I pitch my tent? Where do I find water? Thanks to the Davis family, both needs were met, and it was party time. After I set up my tent in their backyard next to a creek, I hopped in their car and rode with them into town where a festival was set up in a large parking lot. The stage was lit up for live music and food venders lined the edges. Smells of steamy, smoky meat saturated the air. We picked a table and I ventured out for something cold to drink.

I planned for a relaxing evening while in Monticello for Riverfest. I wanted to make more friends and more memories. I was there to pig out on BBQ and cold beer in the company of good people. I wasn't there to have my emotions rocked, but the Davis family would not cooperate.

I returned to the table where Tara and Jillian sat waiting for me. Jordan and her brother Nick were at another table talking with some friends, leaving me a chance to interview Tara. People, for the most part, will come right out and ask the obvious questions, but I was curious about Jordan's story. I wanted to know what this family was going through. Was it manageable to the point where I could hear it, go to sleep, and move on with my life or would it be something that would haunt me in those places inside where others are forbidden to enter? Just let her be OK. She'll go through chemo, lose some hair, endure a few sick days then—Bam! Remission!

Unfortunately, that was not the case. Out of all the places I could have stopped on my 2,400 mile journey down the Mississippi, out of everyone I could have met, I paddled into the land of Jordan Davis.

Jordan is seventeen. At fifteen, she was diagnosed with a rare muscular cancer. I'm not educated enough to know everything about it, but her mother did her best to explain the diagnosis to me, while an 80's cover band blasted *Journey* under the moonlight. She selflessly included me in her daughter's story, going through it with me from beginning to end, reliving the constant fear that they all live with every day. She would talk and I would glance over at Jordan interacting with her brother, Nick, her little sister, Jillian, and all of their friends. I did my best to listen, only to be interrupted with the constant badgering conclusion that this girl had less than a five percent chance of surviving her disease. I understood those odds, however, my medication will keep me in relative health, whereas, she must face a harsh probability.

Tragedy comes in many forms. It may rob like a thief in the night or in the form of a slow lingering "any day now." A short year ago, my family faced tragedy when the doctor at the University of Utah told them their son had forty-eight hours to live, but in reality, I didn't have to face it. I was in a coma. Death could have come and I would never have known. Jordan did not have the comforts of a coma; she faced her mortality every day, standing at the edge of the long night shouting, "Not without a fight!"

Jordan was dealing with more than any teenager should have to endure. And I was angry. Until I met the Davis family, part of my journey was about breaking records and making a name with a puffed chest. After Jordan, that all changed. Meeting her and hearing her story, I could not help feeling like a selfish jackass for complaining about my life. I knew it was not her intention to conjure up such feelings in me. She was the kind of person who wanted those around her to feel nothing but happiness. But the fact remains that I am selfish.

My river was definitely getting the best of me—it was *taking* the best of me. Every day was a reminder that I was still sick as my feet swelled up and my joints throbbed. Some days I woke and wondered what I was really trying to do and why was I doing it on the Mississippi River? What was I running from? What was I running to?

Now, a new question arose: Imagine if I was on the River Jordan?

It put life into a painful simplicity. For her it was about loving and laughing and please, just one more day of living.

I ate, drank, and danced a bit with little Jillian. The festival ended and like many nights before, I was alone in my tent with only my thoughts. There was not much sleep that night. In the house next to my tent lived a family praying for one more day with their loved one.

Something began to stir in me. The change did not happen immediately, but Jordan planted a root that was sure to consume me in the days to come. This journey was not only about me. My brokenness was to bring hope to another, just as Jordan had done for me.

The next morning, after breakfast, it was time to leave the Davis family and lay another thirty miles behind me. We piled in the car and they drove me back to the river's edge and bade me farewell. They took photos with me and Old Blue, then we said our goodbyes. I wanted to tell Jordan that she was the bravest young woman I had ever met, but I may have just whispered it to myself and to the trees.

Typically, whenever departing, I never look back; I simply move on into the unknown, but today I couldn't help myself. I needed to see her once more, standing on the shore, breathing in the new day. I never wanted to forget what true courage looked like.

Jordan died a few months later...

To say, "I was moved by the time I spent with the Davis family on the River Jordan" is a cop-out in my opinion. My heart was wounded because another precious young life has been snuffed out and I was crying out to a silent God for answers. My survival plagued me. Questions of why I survived something so cruel, but she did not, threatens my peace.

I would like to think that whenever I face the battles of life and what it brings and I sit nursing my wounds, I will remember Jordan's struggle and hopefully raise my sword once more and assume my place on the field. Sometimes I wonder if I'll ever get it together. I may fumble and flop the rest of my life traversing a line between selflessness and self-loathing. But there are a couple of things for which I am certain... I will never give up, and my heart was changed because of a young girl by an old river.

Rest on your river, dear Jordan.

RIVER JOURNALL,
JULY 15, 2011

There I was caught up in the scenery, relishing the moments, basking in sunlight, loving my adventure, and singing Everclear's Santa Monica at the top of my lungs. i had my headphones on, so i didn't hear the gang of lively elk River innertubers creeping up behind me. i was so embarrassed but they said, "no! sing more!" We all pulled to shore and they asked of my adventure and shared a beer with me. someday, I'll be home. I'll be at work. I'll be paying bills, and when it gets to be too much, I'll think of this moment and smile.

10

Dear Mom

I am missing you today, Mom.

I met a family, a young girl in particular, who is responsible for changing my motivations behind this adventure. The girl's name is Jordan. She is dying of a rare cancer. They have been on my mind for days. So have you, for you know too well what it's like to fear for the life of your child.

I've been thinking a lot about the man I have become while traversing silently down the Mississippi. Given the childhood that I had, I should have become something more. I am sorry for all of the wasted opportunities.

The slightest things can trigger old memories and it's happened a lot over the last few weeks. Yesterday, I camped near a marina next to some kind-hearted people who shared their breakfast of bagels and cream cheese with me. It made me think of the Wunderbar, that little German eatery in the old Altamonte Mall where you introduced me to bagels and cream cheese for the first time. I think I was seven. After lunch, we would go to that little bakery where they had the most amazing brownies with chocolate frosting on top.

This, of course, triggered more memoires as I placed my SUP in the water for the umpteenth time and set my course south. I know this has been difficult for you. Once a mother, always a mother, right? I'm making my way slowly down the Mississippi. This adventure has been so full of stories and I'm not even half-way home. The Mighty started humbly in the north. She begged me to live in the moment and enjoy the peacefulness of her company. She now roars with power and girth, and has made way for enormous river barges. I am a thumbtack next to them. The lush and wild scenery of the north has receded to make room for civilization, but she is still beautiful nonetheless.

I'm very tired and I hurt a lot, especially in my feet and ankles. It's not the soreness of physical exertion, but the plague of disease. A tale of woe you know all too well. Growing up, I never understood the disease that brought you such pain. I was too self-absorbed to pay attention. People who do not live with constant chronic pain have no idea. They will never understand what it does to a person, not only physically, but mentally as well.

I'm slowly beginning to understand what I will face, and it breaks my heart to know this is what you have endured, on a much deeper level, for most of your life. I may now have a small taste of what you go through physically with cancer, but I'll never be able to comprehend what it was like for you to watch me dying in that hospital bed last year—to see your strong son wither away to nothing. I was asleep through the worst of it, but you endured every creeping minute of anguish that life would leave me at any moment. I'm not a parent, but when I place myself in a similar situation where I had to watch you drift away into death, I can feel the burden in my heart and my stomach begins to ache. I'm so sorry you had to go through that. But I'm alive now, Mom, and I'm trying so hard to live my miracle.

I feel useless sometimes, Mom. What use is there for someone like me in this world? I feel I was born five-hundred years too late.

People like me were great to have around, back when the world was flat, back when the world needed to be explored on mighty ships... then, people needed someone like me. But, what good am I in a modern world?

Sometimes others make me feel bad about my wandering spirit. They say I want to avoid responsibility or I'm having a mid-life crisis. But you know better, don't you? You waved goodbye at the airport when Dad took me to Mexico when I was eight. Ever since then, I've lived in a panic that I would not experience every corner of this magnificent planet before the end. It is so much more than wanderlust; I've been captivated by the unknown. Alas, I still feel bad that I can't seem to find my place. It makes me insecure and sometimes I feel worthless.

Do I make you proud, Mom? When you look back on your legacy as a mother, do I give you a sense of accomplishment, as if maybe you brought a child into this world who could make a difference? I don't feel that I do. I feel like I could have done so much more with the opportunities you provided me. What a selfless job to be a mother. It would take a thousand lifetimes to thank you. If I never had anything in this world and died penniless, I would consider myself a wealthy man for having a mother like you. Honestly, the motivation behind everything I do is to bring pride to you and Dad.

I just wanted you to know I was thinking about you. I'm looking forward to seeing you both in St. Louis. Until then, I love you.

Welcome to the lock, weary traveler.

The Apperts.

Stars of The River Jordan: Jordan, Nick and Jillian Davis.

5-star camping is hard to find.

RIVER JOURNAL,
JULY 26, 2011

I saw her in the distance. Her
vibrant red pigtails beckoned me
to shore. My lust was immediate.
i ached to sink my teeth into her
warm, ample buns. i would drink
from her fountain until my thirst
was quenched and then i would
drink from her once more. i would
take her and make her mine. spicy
chicken combo with a large Dr.
Pepper, please. ah, Wendy's. nice to
see you on the river...

11

Bye Bye Blue

If you find yourself on the river, cruising past Red Wing, Minnesota, do yourself a favor—cross over to Wisconsin and visit the Harbor Bar. Ask for Oompa (like Oompa Lumpa), but only if you have an overwhelming desire to stay in a boiling hot, windowless room for the night. No worries, Oompa. You were only trying to help and you're a hell of a guy. But I'll just stick to my tent. Regardless of the shanty digs, I had a blast at the Harbor Bar.

The sun had set by the time I paddled out of Lock and Dam 3 and then dusk flipped the switch. Night comes quickly in the North. I'm usually out of the water before I need to worry, but the lock took longer than anticipated and I found myself paddling in the dark for the first time since I started my journey.

Nighttime made for tricky navigation on the river and it often leaves a paddler in a state of bewilderment. In fact, river darkness is so black that it's hard to see a hand in front of your face. I felt like I was paddling through outer space amongst the stars. I lost the feel of the river beneath me and began a floating free fall. I fumbled through a dry bag for my headlamp, but all that did was blind me to anything past ten feet. At least before, my eyes had begun to adjust to shadow at shore. Now, it was just black, so away with my lamp.

After an hour paddling in the abyss, I noticed some tiny blinking lights in the distance. I assumed from the lights that it was a barge, but that was just a guess. River barges are quiet in relation to their enormous size. At night, it's hard to gauge from their lights just how close they are. What I could not see, was the bend in the river ahead of me. As I came around the curve, I was no more than twenty yards away from the metal whale. The massive shadow blocked my path to Red Wing. I quickly changed course to avoid a losing battle and wound up on the Wisconsin side. I was too spooked to cross over to Red Wing (the river can be so wide in places it takes me over an hour to paddle across) so I continued to hug the left side in hopes of finding a suitable camp. Wisconsin continued its shroud of darkness while Minnesota teased me with its twinkling lights, but then, like a festive mirage in the desert, the glowing yellow lights of the Harbor Bar came into view.

I paddled to shore, stepped off my board, assuming the ground was solid, and sank past my knees into a beach of stinking, slimy mud. When all I wanted was a nice hot shower, at the end of the day, mud was what I got. While wading through the muck, I noticed that the dark spaces around me looked like a static television screen... then I realized it was filled with flying insects. It was like an Armageddon plague. They turned out to be Mayflies, annoying bugs that only live about a day and leave a putrid smell that would rival any outhouse. There was a trailer home in the woods between me and the Harbor Bar so I dragged my gear through the mud, found a hose, washed up, then strolled into the pub in my bare feet.

Oompa was first to greet me. There were a few scattered patrons about the bar, checking me out as I dripped across the floor, before making myself cozy at the end. I gave introductions and asked Oompa if he served food. He made me a small pizza accompanied with a shot of Jack for the sniffles. I asked him "if and where" I could put a tent up on the property. After I explained what I was doing, I waited for him to stop staring at me like I was a talking squirrel, then Oompa phoned a friend who owned another bar up the road that had a couple of rooms—he'd give me one for ten dollars.

"It's the room the drunks use, so they don't have to drive home," said Oompa.

"Hey, it's a place to sleep that's not a tent."

I was correct, it wasn't a tent. It was a closet with a bed and no windows. It must have been the last stop before hell because it was like a furnace. People were banging on walls, moaning and making sounds that I couldn't attach images to, and I was thankful for that. I have some skills, though. I've become accustomed to sleeping in strange places amongst strange faces for so long, that falling asleep was easy.

The next day, I went back to the Harbor Bar and sat out back on the dock with my feet in the water, trying to decide if it was going to be a day off or a day to move on. That's when I met Aaron and Jodi. They were on their way to a sandbar party in Aaron's boat and invited me to join. Most of the towns I've paddled through have a favorite sandbar that is their weekend party spot. Boats from all around pull up and spend the day grilling, drinking, and whatever else they could conjure up for a mound of dirt in the middle of the river, and the more they drank, the better the ideas got.

Their friends were waiting, so I hopped in the boat and Aaron took off like a maniac. It was the most insane boat ride of my life. My trunks were already wet, so pissing myself wouldn't have mattered. What took me two hours to paddleboard took Aaron ten minutes. At the sandbar, Jodi, Aaron, and all their friends welcomed me as warmly as the sand we stood in. They introduced me, told the group what I was doing, and in minutes I was bathed and fed. Somewhere in the lively chitchat I mentioned that I hadn't showered in a week and before I knew it, Jodi had me in the river with some Dawn (the soap, not a girl), scrubbing away the funk. When I emerged from the river, Aaron handed me a freshly grilled Bratwurst.

It was a good day with more great people.

I ended up staying one more night at the Harbor Bar and enjoyed some live music (one of my favorite things while on an adventure) before leaving yet another amazing town in my wake.

I had to keep paddling, for there was a prize waiting for me in Trempealeau.

ooo

It would be difficult for a person to comprehend the simplicity of the craft I was using for this voyage unless they have had the pleasure of riding a stand-up paddleboard. Three inches of foam and epoxy is all that separated me from the elements. For some stretches of the river there was nothing but the trees and me, and I glided silently through the water as it brought me closer to my Cherokee roots. I'm not full Cherokee, not even half, but the blood is in there and whenever I'm in nature, it bubbles out, bobbling in the breeze.

Paddleboarding exposed me to the natural world unlike anything I had ever experienced before. My SUP made it possible to travel great distances in a minimalistic and intimate way. After five hundred miles, I learned to live on very little and I dropped more unnecessary possessions every day. The little I had was precious to me, and as I watched Old Blue begin to die, it saddened me. He had become my talisman.

He was with me when my legs first began to function once more during rehabilitation.

I remember one particular evening at home, after the hospital. I was staring into the mirror trying to will myself to let go of the walker. Two seconds later, I was on my back on the cold tile floor. So, when paddling Old Blue and my legs burned from an eight hour day on the river, I remember the days of immobility and I did my best to enjoy the pain. Because of my affliction, I will be in pain for the rest of my life... but I can walk. Blue brought me back to the water. But now, I was slowly losing him.

That first day on the river was the beginning of his demise. I patched all the holes as best I could, but for the last five hundred miles water was slipping through the cracks and I struggled with every pull of the paddle. My rails were in deep and the water lapped over my feet. It was exhausting, brutal paddling, but I was going down with the ship. Every day I prepared myself for the board to give way and crack in the center. Each day it would sink a little more. I knew our journey was ending, despite my desire to move forward.

From the beginning of the odyssey, my dad had been posting updates, calling news stations and doing whatever he could to promote my trip. He knew how strongly I felt about raising money to donate to the hospital. Every dime people gave went to the charity on my website. I had my own cash, I ate cans of ravioli, filled up my water with garden hoses, and accepted the kindness of strangers. If someone wanted to give me money, as they did through seemingly every town I passed, I would tell them to go onto the website and click the donate button. I may have been a deathbed survivor, who turned into a depressed lump of crap, but I was going to raise money for the hospital. I didn't care how small the amount. However, I had no extra funds and no sponsorship. When my SUP went down, I would follow, and the journey would be over.

But it was not to be.

To say I'm a blessed man is an understatement. My life is full of with beautiful family and friends. When word got out that I was struggling, so many came to my aid. My dad posted about my struggles on Facebook and my friends rallied. But the true facilitator of good fortune, the one who made continuing my journey possible, would be my friend Debbie Blunt. Debbie was friends with the owners of YOLO paddleboards, Jeff Archer and Tom Losee. She called them and told them what I was doing and they were more than happy to sponsor me with a new fourteen-foot YOLO SUP so I could complete my journey. All I had to do was sign it when I returned home, so they could put it on their wall inside the paddleboard shop.

I've heard it said before... "If you try and do good things, good things will come your way." I never imagined the payback would be so generous. People were giving me so much more than I could ever give them in return. With the paddleboard secured, my friends turned their attention to delivery. Debbie stepped up once more and selflessly volunteered to drive it to Nashville where she would hand it off to my good friend James. (He's always up for a road trip). He would then carry the torch from Tennessee to Wisconsin. We estimated travel times, and Trempealeau, Wisconsin, seemed to be the best fit. I was closing in on two months without a familiar face so I was excited for my friend to arrive.

I moved on from Red Wing and set my sights on Trempealeau. My goal for the day was Lake City but hellacious headwinds fought against every inch paddled. By early afternoon, I was parched and famished. I never replenished food and water supplies in Red Wing, assuming I would reach Lake City in reasonable amount of time. My stomach gnawed at my ribs and my throat felt like sandpaper. I was on the verge of gulping river water when Jason and Dawn pulled alongside me in their cabin cruiser. They were out with some friends doing what people do on the river, having a good time and like many before, they were curious about the weird guy on the floating log. They pulled me on board, tied my SUP to the back, and stuffed me with spicy chicken pasta and all the water I could drink. Jason wanted to tow me into Lake City, but I made him promise to circle in the same area that I pulled out.

There were three primary reasons for me being on the river: to tell my story, to heal my spirit, and to raise money for the hospital so others suffering can share in the same generosity that I received. Like many times before, I would talk and people were moved, but when the tears started to fall, that's when I begin to realize the true impact that it had on others. Dawn wiped her cheeks and I felt bad for upsetting her. It was never my intention; I simply wanted people to understand the miracle of my survival.

After an hour with my new friends, I was back in the water with a wave and a smile. Black clouds loomed behind me. I was having such a good time with Jason and Dawn; I failed to notice the storm's proximity.

Lake City borders Lake Pepin. I was hoping to make it into town, but with the approaching thunderstorm, I needed to get off the river. I set up camp on a small peninsula just north of Lake City and battened down the hatches for the night. The rains came in a fury and lasted well into the evening. I fell asleep to the pitter-patter and woke up at five in the morning in a puddle of water with a collapsed tent on top of me. Exhausted and pissed off, I loaded my soggy gear on Old Blue and he sank under the weight. I left the peninsula, entered Lake Pepin, and after spending an hour trying to kill a short distance of a few hundred yards, I got out at Lake City, dragged Old Blue and my gear across the highway and checked into a hotel. It was heaven. I had a hot shower, a soft bed, and I washed clothes that hadn't seen the inside of a washing machine for weeks.

Lake City was another quaint, pleasurable river town. I enjoyed the difference in perspective when entering a place from the water as opposed to land. Most people I talked with expressed a desire to leave, but for someone paddling in, it's the only place they want to be. If you find yourself passing through Lake City, stop off at Skyline. It's a great little bar/restaurant on the water. Ask for Holly. Tell her Mississippi Matt says "Hello!"

Clean, fed, and well rested, I moved on from Lake City and set my sights on Wabasha, but barely made it halfway. My dear SUP was rapidly dying and it was making me sad. It may seem silly, but your vessel becomes a part of you. However, my love for Old Blue was coupled with frustration. It took two strokes to move a yard. It would be easier to walk on water than to paddle another mile. And then, to add to an already difficult situation, I lost my damn paddle.

I took several breaks throughout the day; thanks to the fatigue produced by a water logged SUP. I was conversing with some people hanging out at another sandbar and simply didn't notice that my paddle had come loose and set sail for New Orleans without me. I kept a collapsible kayak paddle strapped to the bow for emergencies; it would get me to my new board, but it was just another thorn in my side.

My lack of desire to get back on the river must have been obvious to Kevin and Jenny because they invited me to come back up river to Bass Camp for dinner. Bass camp was a home-away-from-home for their group. A place for friends and family to get away, play on the river, build bonfires, and enjoy life. Kevin's buddy, Rich, said I could crash with him in his RV, so we loaded up my gear and were on our way.

There was a buffet already prepared and waiting. One would have to spend eight hours paddling in the sun to appreciate the elation that comes when kind people pluck you from the water and sit you down in front of a smorgasbord of fish and salads. While I feasted, the girls of Bass Camp asked me more questions in an hour than most did in a week! But they were very sweet girls, and I'll always remember them with fondness.

The fire was roaring and the kids took turns standing by my SUP and snapping pictures. I kept a Sharpie with me so everyone I met could sign the board. Kevin told me to join him and Jenny in their golf cart and they gave me the royal tour of the campgrounds.

Whenever these experiences find me, they fill me with warmth, and I think it has something to do with the subconscious connection we all have as a global family.

Stories of violence and pain saturate our daily lives. We are a media-driven society and we have allowed the digital negativity to corral us into a false sense of apprehension and fear. I don't know much about anything. I'm not an authority on all things human, but I've spent the last four years on the road in some fashion or another. I rode my motorcycle through forty-four states, sampling cites large and small from Maine to Arizona. I've hitchhiked hundreds of miles and shared time with countless strangers, and I will never believe there is more evil than good. There *is* great evil in this world, no doubt about it, but it is not the majority, and love remains the unseen force that binds us. Not everyone on the river invites me into their lives and extends the red carpet, but they are kind and respectful and that will bridge anyone together. The majority of people I've encountered just wanted to live and let live. They wanted to feed their dogs, play with their kids, go to work, pay the bills, and be at peace. Maybe they don't have the same philosophies or beliefs as I do, but why should that matter? Humanity is like a massive marriage of souls. We can choose to be petty and pick on the little things or we can look deeper, be patient, and focus on the good in others. It's there if you are willing to open your heart more than your eyes. I realize my philosophies lean towards a utopian way of thinking, but what good ever comes from being negative all the time?

There are those who accuse me of being naive and that eventually, if I don't keep the world at arm's length and protect myself, the unimaginable will happen. Well, the unimaginable has happened, more than once, and yet I am still here. It is my hope that, besides my story of death and rehabilitation, the people I encounter will also strive to see the best in their global brothers and sisters.

Early the next day, the Bass Camp clan took me back to the exact spot where they had picked me up. After photos and hugs, we parted ways. I wonder if I left them the way they left me: full of hope and smiles.

Two days later, I floated into Trempealeau on four flat tires. Old Blue was finished. James was on his way with my new SUP and I was excited, but it was coupled with sadness as I laid my partner to rest.

I'll miss you, Blue.

I paddled to the left of Lock and Dam 6 and entered a marina adorned with boats. While dragging my gear to shore, a very pregnant mommy-to-be and her husband were on their way to the family houseboat for some dinner and downtime. Her husband must have left something in the car because he did a one-eighty and headed back towards the parking lot; her path continued its course towards mine. As I passed, gear in tow, she started up a conversation with me and invited me to join them for dinner. Jason, her husband, returned and we made introductions, but when his wife informed him that I was coming aboard for steak, he turned three shades of "who the hell is he and why is he joining us?" I could tell he just wanted to be alone with his wife and have a relaxing meal. Normally, I would have made an excuse to duck out and let them be, but something told me that Jason and I were going to get along.

It took about fifteen minutes. The friendship was solidified, and Jason made it his mission to see that my stay in Trempealeau was the best it could possibly be. Jason was a dairy farmer and he invited me to stay with his family at the farm. I protested and told him that I had imposed on them enough. Besides, James was coming with my board and I had to hang close to shore. Jason graciously accepted my refusal and took me to the Historic Trempealeau, a wonderfully cozy B&B on the river, and introduced me to the owner. He told her what I was doing and her eyes lit up. Her son was hiking the Pacific Rim and had written home about all types of random acts of kindness. So, what did she do? She gave me a room for two nights. Free of charge.

"We are just paying it forward," she smiled as warmly as only a mother could.

I asked Jason if he'd mind me tagging along with him the next day so I could see how a real dairy farm worked. He was more than happy to oblige and promised to pick me up in the morning.

"Please, no farmer's hours," I smiled.

We said goodbye and I went to check out my new digs. The room was beyond amazing. It was so quaint and cozy, I wanted to return in the winter, build a fire, and write a book about the river.

While relaxing in my free room, I called James. He would be leaving in the morning from Nashville and would be driving all day so I had time to kill. I caught up on some writing and then, as promised, Jason picked me up the next day and gave me the grand tour of his dairy farm. The whole day was an eye opening education into what an American farmer goes through to provide us with sustenance. I witnessed the local vet, elbow deep into an artificial insemination of a black and white bovine, followed up by a steak dinner with Jason's family.

The following morning, I got a text that the coming of Miss Sunshine was at hand (my new SUP already had a name). I bounced down the hotel stairs, out the front door and into a big hug from my buddy James.

James is my soul brother. The kind of friend that just *gets* you without having to discuss who you are. When I was on my motorcycle adventure in 2008, he welcomed me into his home in Nashville for a few days and I've never had more fun just hanging with someone and talking about anything and nothing.

Miss Sunshine was bungeed, strapped, and duct taped to the top of his car in a proficiently haphazard manner. He delivered her to me unharmed and she was beautiful. The SUP could easily carry an additional fifty pounds over what I already had. It was going to be a nice float to New Orleans.

James, and his two friends that had tagged along to keep him company, were famished after their sixteen-hour road trip so I offered to buy them some breakfast. We had coffee and some catch-up time, and then he informed me that he was going to hit the road immediately after his cup reached dry bottom. I was disappointed, to say the least. I had hoped for more time. It was a mission of mercy, his bringing me the board, but I just wanted some familiar company, board or not. But James had things to do and places to be, and I understood without words because that is how we understand each another—without words. So, I hugged him tight and waved goodbye while standing lonely in the middle of 3rd Street.

On my third and final day in Trempealeau, Farmer Jason and his family came out to watch me launch. I had my beautiful new SUP, courtesy of YOLO paddleboards, packed and ready for launch. I was starting to look like a professional, and my gear was now at the caliber of my paddling competitors. Unfortunately, quality equipment came too late as far as placing first was concerned.

Back when I had discovered that I would not be the first to accomplish a journey by SUP down the Mississippi River, I was distraught to say the least. I was stripped of something that nobody had and nobody could take away. Records can be broken, but nobody can ever take away the accomplishment of being first. But things were changing inside of me. After spending the last two months sharing time with the amazing people of the river and stockpiling remarkable stories in heart and on paper, I discovered peace that I was where I was supposed to be in this river race: In third place, amongst friendship and love sharing my story of hope. It's the only place I wanted to be, until my river reaches the end of all things.

RIVER JOURNAL,
AUGUST 1, 2011

Just dodged a hail storm by a matter of minutes. i could see the plopping golf balls approaching from the other side of the river. i made it to the dock and into a cozy tavern called The Cove with hail on my heels. Cozy taverns on a rainy day. Feels so medieval...

12

The Detour

The day began in a sluggish funk. Old demons again. My loneliness was visiting more often as my journey ambled along the banks of the Mighty Miss. I walked a fine line between enjoying my alone time and craving togetherness, but, truth be told, it is togetherness that called to me the most.

I had been on The Mighty for more than forty days and some odd nights. Iowa was slowly approaching. It was like a carrot dangling in front of an ass. I made my way from Trempealeau, past La Crosse, and into Brownsville, Minnesota where I paddled past a manufactured cove and noticed several boats beached on its shore. I could hear the music pumping and I would have liked to stop. *I should have stopped*, I told myself. Instead, I dug my heels deeply into my melancholy day and continued for another five miles. I've been to other sandbar parties before. I was determined to make it to Iowa. I needed to make Iowa. I needed to feel as if I had accomplished something new amidst the old routine.

I almost quit after my first day on the Mississippi, but after pushing through the defeat, I made a promise to finish Minnesota. Barring a head-on collision with a tugboat, I was going to enter the great state of Iowa, come hell or no water—I'd drag my board across mud if I had to.

Past Brownsville, the river would widen, and I would enter Lock and Dam 8, next to Genoa. Beyond that, Iowa. Beyond that? Maybe home. There was always a weakness in me that wanted to go home. My body throbbed from head to foot. Some days I almost felt like my old self again, and then my disease reminded me that I will never be my old self again. My joints and muscles glowed orange with fire, like a blacksmith was pounding at them with his hammer. When I jumped in the river to cool off, I could almost hear them hiss and spew steam like a teakettle. I mentally patted myself on the back and gave myself reassurance that after this dam, I had at least finished Minnesota.

The river opened north of Genoa. Tugboats tugged and recreational boats scurried by me pointing and waving.

There is the dam, possibly no more than an hour's paddle.

That's when they showed up.

They came upon me with such merriment and open arms and I went to war inside my heart for maybe a second. Should I turn up my music? Should I pretend I don't see them? I'm finally making some headway and now these people want a story. Look at the lonely man and his tomfoolery... he's good for a laugh.

Had I known who they were-had I known *what* they were-I would have been searching for them around every curve and in every bend. Maybe I already was, deep down in places where I don't allow most people to visit. Maybe I needed them at that exact moment. And, in that exact moment, they were there. I did not need them until they came to be and when they appeared, I wondered how I did without them this long.

I remember David first. He called down to me from the roof of the houseboat, "Would you like a beer?" And right then, David made me part of the family.

They were from Iowa, all ten of them, five sets of middle-Americans sailing on fresh waters under blue skies. The houseboat approached and from the top, they waved and cheered like angels from Heaven sent to comfort a weary traveler.

David was tall, powerful and lively. His voice boomed and his kindness pierced through me like rays from the sun. He, along with his friends, Jim and Matthew, helped me aboard and tied Miss Sunshine to the deck. Danielle offered to make me a sandwich, "Little Danielle" they called her, and she smiled like a summer sun shower. Matthew immediately engaged me in conversation and making a new friend as easily as most gather air, and there you have a taste of three of them.

In a lickety split, we were on our way to I don't know where, and I found myself on the roof of the boat in the midst of true warmth, and it's not the sun I speak of. It was the warmth of selflessness. Two cowboy hats sat to my right and the people living under them were Jim and Cat. I felt as if I was their brother the moment they began speaking to me, and it confuses me how effortlessly it came to be.

The festive crew, my captains of detour, took me back up river to the very cove I desired to visit, and for two days, they shared their lives with me. They shared everything with me, heart and soul, food and wine. This was their time. Their time away from the things of man and everyday life. Their time to let loose, and they gave it to me.

For two days they paraded me around and Matthew introduced me to anyone he could, even if they were strangers, just to tell my story. These people would not allow an event to take place without including me. When my hands were empty, they made sure they were overflowing, and I wondered to myself how many pass them by and never see kindness in their open arms.

We paddled together; we shared stories and meals. I spent forty-eight straight hours with my detour, and in that time they became everything I needed and something I will never be able to let go.

I was in love with my new houseboat family, and they were so in love with each other that it reminded me of what I would never find. It brought me to rage as the tick tock of every day passes, and it never got better. It will never get better. I was broken before and I was broken still. I made it sound as if this were a noble quest to pay it forward, but it seemed, at this point, to have ulterior motives... dark in meaning. I lost someone who was a like a brother to me. He died and I wasn't there. One month later, I fell into a coma and before the year was up, someone who I thought cared for me decided that a rehabilitating man was too much to bother with, and she left me as if I were nothing more to her than a stranger in a crowd. Hopelessness is why I was there on that river. And if there was hope, it was that I never made it home. I wanted to become comfortably numb. I needed a new temptation to lead me down a different path. That very night, my new temptation presented herself, and I was ready to exploit the opportunity and take a step to the other side.

But as it came to pass, my detour entered a fork in the road, and I tested the waters. I met a crew a few boats away, a young lady in particular, the kind of woman who could make you forget.

Two boats beached in the cove, and I'm sorry I could not travel both. She came to our fire on that second night, and I left my new family by the warmth and followed her flames into the night. She brought me back to her boat where a new party had formed. Shots and smoke, and my head was spinning drunk. Their faces changed in the shadows. What do I owe them back home? What do I owe any of them? I grow weary of my story. I grow weary of this "miracle," title that they label me. I am no miracle! I'm a fool. I strive for a life of kindness and friendship. I try to do the right thing, but the wrong thing consumes me, and buries me deep underground. What if I allow myself to venture to the point of no return, a place where the good in me is abolished and I can live out the rest of my days calloused and unaffected by the actions of others? No more, "Love one another." Love me, only me.

She placed an object on her tongue and slipped it in my mouth then wrapped her arms around me. Sometimes there are things you do, things you see, things you become part of and they alter your perception forever. They alter your attitude. They desensitize you to things that once made you feel sensitive, and I knew after her they would all be different. After that night, on her boat, I would step off in the morning a new man. A darker man.

And then, the voice returned.

"Move from this place."

It was the same voice that spoke to me in my coma. The voice on the Wekiva telling me to pay it forward. It angered me as it persisted.

"You are not finished."

I hung my head and my arms released her. This wasn't me... this can't be what I have become. I stood up and left her in the dark, along with my chance to erase all compassion in my heart. I left her confused and retreated into the night.

As I stumbled off the boat into the blackness, feet crunching sand, towards my little tent on the hill, I could hear my detour in the distance. Their laughter and sweet voices were riding the cool breeze and descending upon my war. I went to them and opened my heart. I brought them into places that are dark and covered with cobwebs... and they listened.

I sat there under the stars with them and let them become part of me. It was time. Somebody needed to hear what my hurt sounds like. Only time knew which ears my woes should fall upon.

Andy made me laugh non-stop since the moment I had met him, and then Andy became something more. Slurred words became a soothing balm because it flowed from one of the biggest hearts I had ever met, and I understood the meaning behind everything he said to me. Casey reminded me of a dear friend I had grown up with who could speak such comfort. I'm sure she doesn't even know how comforting she can actually be. Nick rarely spoke to me because he knew how to listen and if you think about it, that is a lost art and hard to cultivate. He listened and only said things that needed to be said.

Jim and Cat shared their pain from past days. There is something unique in the sound of a person's voice when they reflect on great sorrow they have endured and I could hear it in theirs. They gave me hope for the future, knowing their children would one inherit the world. This could be said for all my new friends raising selfless versions of themselves to go forth and combat evil.

As I spoke and choked back my tears, I felt a new freedom fall upon me, and the stars began to glow through the clouds once again. Tomorrow, I was certain to paddle into better days.

The next morning, my beloved tribe of house-boating hoodlums took me back to the spot upriver where they picked me up two days prior. I followed them into Lock and Dam 8 located in Genoa, Wisconsin, and trailed behind towards the coveted Iowa border. Minnesota produced a healthy dose of life-altering memories and gave me some of my most precious stories. But I was ready for a new state, and in just a few more miles, I would have it.

The clan told me to meet them at a small campground where they would spend one last night on the houseboat before returning home. When the day ended and the mid-western sun tucked itself behind the horizon, they saw me approaching from far off, and began to cheer. "Welcome to Iowa!"

I shared a final breakfast with them and we said our goodbyes. As I floated away, I waved, looking over my shoulder only once, taking a final snapshot to place in my mental scrapbook.

A life lived without togetherness is no life at all. That is what my detour taught me. My new friends had experienced great pain; they have walked where I have walked, but instead of living in past shadows, they plan future parties. I hope they think of me from time to time as I make my way downriver and saunter along dusty roads through everyday America.

I will never forget them. Of this, I am certain.

ooo

Days rambled slowly and methodically through Lansing, Prairie Du Chien, Clayton, and finally into Guttenberg where I had a bed waiting thanks to my detour friends. As I paddled through a side slough into Guttenberg, the sun dripped into dusk behind me and fell to places I have not seen or may have seen and forgotten. I suppose wherever the sun drips, there is the same mixture of comings and goings in other lands.

My competition has far since left me in their wake. Alex will soon reach river's end, and Dave has put hundreds of miles between us. As they scoop up popularity and press, I'm left behind in the shadows. However, I can say with sincerity, all is good in the water and the woods.

It was around these lonely but reflective days, soon after crossing the Minnesota/Iowa border that I began talking to a girl online, and the attraction to her increased as I moved from Guttenberg towards Dubuque, Iowa. I anticipated many things on the river: cold nights, loneliness, hunger, and a host of unforeseen dangers, but I never anticipated Cora.

Before I left for the Mississippi, I was rooming with my childhood friend, Jenny. It was on her Facebook page that I first noticed Cora. I soon found that Jenny wasn't my only lifelong friend that Cora knew. I should have met her a thousand times already. I'd lived within a few miles of her for the last ten years. My best friend from kindergarten had his 30th birthday at her house.

Just like my illness, Cora came out of nowhere. I don't care much for social networks. I use them, but I would prefer face-to-face contact, and I certainly wouldn't fall for someone through one. Would I?

Whenever I made it to a little town for the night, I would set up camp, then find somewhere to plug in my computer (I had a small laptop stuffed in three dry sacks) so that I could journal about the day and place a new chapter in the book. When I was through with my words about the river, I would wander over to Facebook and see what was new with Cora. She would make a funny comment on a mutual friend's page and I would try to think of a clever way to direct a jab towards her. I guess it worked because before long, we became friends. The verdict is still out as to who requested whom, but she'll say it was me, and she's probably right. I was captivated with her and I was going to know her.

Cora was a traveler and a photographer. I was immediately attracted to her photography. Something was unique about the way she took pictures. I think it was the way she saw people. She had a gift for capturing their essence through a lens. She photographed people the way I tried to write about them.

For several weeks, we ping-ponged back and forth in a flirtatious cyber dance. I loved her humor; it was sassy with just the right amount of raunch. She was always happy and playful. Her infectious spirit was contagious, even via the internet. She followed my river adventure and I just followed her.

But then, one day, there was sorrow in her status. I settled in for the night, after another thirty-mile day, and maintained my routine by setting up camp, downing a can of ravioli, then wandering the streets in search of a coffee shop.

I was anticipating another humorous update from her—she seemed to have a knack for attracting the weird in her day-to-day life—but that night I found her status to be more melancholy in nature. I sat staring at the screen, clicking my fingernails against the oak table in the coffee shop. "Should I write her?" I thought. I told myself that I wasn't significant enough in her life to make an impact on her and I was also concerned that I would come across stalkerish by writing something too personal to someone I had never met. In the end, I did what I always do and jumped in headfirst.

I took a chance and wrote her a private message, something encouraging. I don't have an abundance of great qualities, but I can write a letter. I think it had the right effect because from then on, I seemed to have become more to her.

Shortly after my letter, the texting began, which quickly turned into a phone call. I liked that about her—taking it from the impersonal to the personal. That first phone call lasted an hour. I can't remember everything about the conversation because I was so shy and nervous that I could only hear my heartbeat in my ears.

Apparently, a year before, she was having dinner with one of our mutual friends, Kim. It was during my "deathbed" time. Kim was confiding in Cora and telling her how upset she was because I was about to die, to which, Cora replied, "No, I don't feel like that is what is going to happen. I don't think he is going to die. I believe that life has more in store for him." Now, fast forward a year later, I'm alive and she was quickly becoming a big part of my journey.

The kindness in Cora's words during our phone calls meant more to me than I allowed her to know. Walls were collapsing at the hands of gentleness. The more we talked on the phone, day after day, the more my desire for something more than friendship began to surface. Two things in particular prompted the transformation.

The first was a quote she posted on my page by Elisabeth Kübler-Ross. It was after I wrote my letter of encouragement to her.

"The most beautiful people we have known are those who have known defeat, known suffering, known struggle, known loss, and have found their way out of the depths. These persons have an appreciation, a sensitivity, and an understanding of life that fills them with compassion, gentleness, and a deep loving concern. Beautiful people do not just happen."

I remember reading it and feeling my eyes well up. I didn't feel like a beautiful person, but she was slowly changing the way I viewed myself.

The second was in reference to my journey: She told me that whenever she thought of the river and of me, she saw three lights paddling south. The first light was Alex, the second light was Dave and I was a distant third. She explained that she would see this vision as if she was looking at a map with a tracker device on all of us. The lights were paddling south on the map toward the Gulf of Mexico. She said my light was slow and wandering, but it was by far the brightest.

"You're flirting with me," I smiled into the phone.

"No", she said, "this is what I see. I believe it means that even though you are not the first person on this journey, it will be your story that will live far beyond the river's end. Your story will reach many. So, don't worry if you are not the first person to finish, this isn't the goal I see for you. I see it is about the people. It is about you healing. It is about your story encouraging others along the way that there is hope and hearing their stories in return. It is about you dropping off your baggage with each stroke and learning to believe in yourself again."

After that day, our phone conversations were two or more hours for the next month and by the time I paddled into Dubuque, exactly two months into my journey, I had plans to meet this lady on the river.

I had a place to stay in Galena with a fellow named Andrew Van Osdol. During my motorcycle road trip a couple years back, I landed a job working security at the Sundance Film Festival in Park City, Utah, at a place called The Star Bar. It was there that I met my buddy Thad.

I love those kinds of people who have a gift for the basics: I'm thirsty, so you give me drink. I'm hungry, so you feed me. I need a place to sleep and you provide a pillow. It comes so easy to some. Thad gave me a place to stay in Utah and I guess he wanted to continue his tradition of finding refuge for me, so he took it upon himself to secure lodging on the river. Enter Andy Van Osdol, friend of Thad, a resident of Galena, provider of Matt's pillow.

Andy had a cabin off a slough that you could only reach by boat (obviously, not a problem for me). I had a TV interview in Dubuque and then I pushed for Galena where I would spend the next two days hanging with Andy. His cabin was in a haunting setting, tucked off the river on stilts, ripe for a spooky story, but I stayed off my pen and chose, instead, to goof off with Mr. Van O. We grilled out, chilled out, and then he took me into town to see some live music later that night. Besides meeting people, live music is another favorite pastime on the road or the river. I told him about the girl who was thinking about flying from Florida to Iowa to kayak next to me for two weeks.

"She's a photo girl, like you. I mean, she's a photographer like you... not that you're a girl." "Nice," Andy smiled.

The next day we wandered around Chestnut Ski Resort and I experienced the amazing Alpine Slide. I really enjoyed hanging out with him. We slipped into friendship quite comfortably and I probably would have spent another day fraternizing with Andy, but I had a date with a lady in Davenport.

And you mustn't keep a lady waiting.

Tumbleweed, Jim Dandy and Miss Sunshine.

My Detour.

Traffic

RIVER JOURNAL,
AUGUST 8, 2011

Ben! Crazy man of the river, time
for you to break free and take
an adventure. or not. Hanging
out with you and your boys was
epic. Wish i could have kept the
moonshine jug, though. listen,
man, life is short and we only
get one shot. Make it count! Get
on that rope swing of life and
Tarzan your ass into the great
unknown!

13

Angels in the Night

Nights in the hospital were my least favorite part of the day. Every moment that I remember was like something out of a nightmare, so it's like choosing a slap in the face or a punch in the gut, but looking back on the experience in its entirety, nighttime was the worst.

During the day, my mom and dad would stand bedside, catering to my every whim—helping me move my arms and legs, scratching that itch on my nose—and reassuring me that I wasn't going to regress and bleed to death. It was difficult to believe them. Their faces still bore the lines that formed while witnessing their child struggling to live in the ICU for sixteen days.

I did my best to sleep during the day in between dialysis treatments and blood transfusions. I had an IV burst in my right arm, and it felt like someone broke my wrist with a hammer. I received a drug called Dilauded through IV, and it was definitely the "high" point of my day. The liquid hospital heroin would travel up my left arm warm and tingly, cross over my chest, and then back down my right arm, snuffing out the pain like a flood washing over the earth. In a matter of minutes, I was snoring.

The only drawback, it had a short shelf life and two hours later, I was awake again. It was also highly addictive. Eventually, I was weaned off my liquid lover.

My daily routine kept me somewhat busy. Mornings began with the doctor's rounds and the reading of test results, more needles, dialysis, medications, then attempting to lift my feet an inch off the bed, PT torture, orders to choke down six awful protein shakes a day and then, before I knew it, darkness fell, blotting out the warm light filtering through the window in my room. Reluctantly, my exhausted parents would leave me in the care of the nurses and retire to their hotel across the street. There I would lie, propped against pillows, alone and quiet, consumed with fear that my heart was going to stop or my head would bleed out of every hole.

Nobody could give me a straight answer when I inquired about my mortality. I would ask, "Is it possible that I could shut down again? Could my organs quit? Will I bleed out again?" To which I would receive a generic response such as, "You are young. You have that going for you."

Nighttime hours were twice as long as they were during the day. I hated bothering the nurses for every minor discomfort, so I'd lie there and force myself not to think about how bad my nose itched or how frustrating it was knowing that I couldn't even turn my own body. The more I would try to ignore it, the worse it would get, and the tears would trickle down my face. I couldn't do a damn thing for myself. I'd watch the clock with its second hand waving like a middle finger, tick-tocking and mocking by waving its collection of fat lazy a.m. hours in my face.

Night after night in a dimly lit room, I listened to the same hums and beeps. Sometimes, somebody would code in a room near me and I'd watch through the tiny rectanglular window in my door as nurses would flash by in a flurry of white, pink and sea-green scrubs. Whenever I was lucky enough to fall asleep, I'd have a nightmare that my face was gushing blood. My parents told me that while I was in the coma, they couldn't stop the blood from pouring out of my ears, nose and eyes, so I suspect that is where my nightmares found their genesis. It wasn't their fault. I wanted to know what happened during the sixteen days that were stolen from me.

One evening in particular, I drifted off and the IV in my arm moved ever so slightly. I still had a very low platelet count, so when I woke up, I discovered a warm, wet sensation tickling my lower back and found that my arm was gummed up in a puddle of blood. Imagine having a nightmare that you are bleeding to death, then waking up to a very real pool of blood under you, and not be able to lift a finger to push the button and alert the nurse.

Helplessness. I never understood the emotional enslavement that word was embodied before.

There is a reason I am sharing this intense hatred for the night. I hated nights in the hospital with all the fear and anger within me, boiling out of every pore, both merging to create a single beast of emotion, and I've hated them ever since. Because with the night came the nightmares, cracked eyes, and acidic stomach pains. There was no relief and, eventually, I surrendered myself to the night and all it held.

But, that's over now.

ooo

By my second month on the river, I found a new love for the night. Every day I would eagerly await the dusk to slip into darkness because when the night came, I was bundled in my tent recouping from another ten-hour paddle.

It was time to talk to Cora.

I'm not sure what made her my angel of night. I had met

other girls on the river, girls who showed obvious interest, but I always floated away without so much as a glance over my shoulder. We talk to thousands of people in our lifetime. Why one in particular can have such a profound effect in such a short time will have to remain a mystery, I guess.

Cora brought peace to the silent evenings, resting alone in my tent, and the days following our talks were brighter than the others. I know firsthand how deep the darkness of night can be. When I journeyed through my valley of shadows during my hospital stay, my eyes matured and I learned to allow my soul to bathe in the warmth and vivid color of a new dusk before the sun could set, and it was lights out in my prison cell once more. Cora broke through those walls of fear that entombed me as if they were made of dandelions, scattering their fluffy white clocks into the wind. Now, she was on her way to meet me face to face and spend the next two weeks in a kayak beside me on the Mighty.

To tell you a bit about Cora, she was an avid world traveler. Her companions were her backpack, laptop, and camera. She had experience in the art of traveling and visited nine Asian countries back in 2008, so I knew she could fend for herself. Her friends, Michelle and Pujan, owned a hotel in Nepal and threw out an invite to return, but that's when I came along and dropped a subtle invitation to join me for a week on the river. Thankfully, she picked the corn-fed state of Iowa over the exotic splendor of Nepal, but it seemed that getting to Davenport would prove to be a more challenging destination. The cost of a plane ticket into an airport close to Davenport was outrageous. I told Cora to research other airports within a few hours distance from the Quad Cities. She found a reasonable one-way fare into Cedar Rapids, only a couple of hours away.

The problem with this destination, once she arrived, was how would she get to Davenport? There was no ground transportation available, like a bus. A taxi would have been too expensive, as would renting a car one-way, so I offered to hitchhike to the airport, pick her up, and then we could thumb it together back to the river. This idea was less than appealing to her.

On August 13, I would meet my new friend for the first time. She would be spending her birthday with me in the Quad Cities. The pressure was on to make it a night she would remember for years upon years to come. To add to the intimidation, two of her best friends from high school would be driving over from her hometown in Chicago for the birthday festivities. I took inventory of what I had to offer: A paddleboard, a bag of dirty clothes, no place to sleep, and the task of making a good impression on a girl I had never met *and* her best friends.

Along route to the Quad-Cities, I stopped just north of Davenport at a little town called Le Clair. I'm beginning to sound like a broken record, but Le Clair is definitely one of my favorite river destinations. The town was setting up for Tug Fest. At the end of this particular festival, they would stretch a rope across the river and there would be a tug of war match between Le Claire and Port Byron. I found a beautiful green patch near the edge of town and set up my tent by the river, just past the carnival rides. My initial thought was to crash a bit and read a book in the shade, but it was such a beautiful day—the kind of day where the weather is so perfect that it actually motivates you—so I decided to walk the town from one end to the next.

At the town's center, there was a map posted on a bulletin board that listed all the local attractions. I ran my finger down rows of shops, restaurants, and points-of-interest. About halfway down the list, I came to a screeching halt, followed by an expression of disbelief.

There have been few moments in my life when the

magnificence of coincidence was so huge that it left me feeling flush with a shot of giddy. La Claire was one of those moments; and to think I might have floated by, oblivious to the kismet. They were here, and they had no idea what they did for me. I spoke briefly about nights in the hospital, but failed to mention two characters that kept me company in the twilight hours, making the time more bearable. It was tough to find something to watch on TV that could help divert my mind from thoughts of death, but I could always count on Mike Wolfe and Frank Fritz from the show *American Pickers* to provide me with a warm televised embrace. Mike and Frank were on TV when I needed them most. They became my two-dimensional friends. I loved watching them scour the country for treasure and I shared their passion for the find. In some ways, they gave me inspiration to seek a treasure of my own, if only internally.

I stood frozen with my index finger glued to the plastic cover, directly over the spot where the words AMERICAN PICKERS were etched on the map. I pulled out my phone to call Cora. I wanted to share this insane conversion of cosmic forces that brought me to this place, but she didn't answer. So I made my way up Hwy. 67 to Davenport Street, and as I rounded the corner, past the BP gas station, I saw the old Studebaker followed by the famous van with the words *Antique Archeology* painted on the side.

The very sight warmed my heart.

I anticipated that Mike and Frank would not be there, but it didn't matter. The connection of coincidence and seeing the shop was good enough for me. Someday, maybe I'll have a chance to tell them in person that they spent time with a very sick man in a hospital and put a smile on his bloated face. The story would've been better had they actually been there, subconsciously waiting for me to arrive, but I would rather think of them on the road, searching for their next treasure because that's exactly what I was doing. Only my road was a river, and I would soon discover a treasure of immeasurable worth.

The next morning, I broke camp and waved goodbye to Le Clair with a big smile on my scruffy face. Two months ago, I was drowning in depression. Now, I was floating down a river teeming with life. I was revitalized, and I couldn't wait for Cora to arrive so I could share some river time with her. I didn't know how, but I was going to give her the birthday of a lifetime.

I had less than twenty-four hours to get to Davenport, hide my board, find a place for the birthday girl and friends, and get to the airport. Some boaters in Le Claire told me the marina outside the Isle of Capri Casino Resort might let me hide my board while I hitchhiked into Cedar Rapids. I thanked them as I floated away, and a few hours later, I docked in Davenport. The boaters described the casino and marina to me; said there was no way I could miss it as long as I kept a look out for the big bridge spanning the river. The casino would be just before it. I hugged the west side of the river until the overpass came into sight and drifted over to the dock. I tied up my board, walked up to the bar at the marina, and pleaded my case to the bartender. He did what he could for me, but in the end, his superiors simply would not allow me to leave my paddleboard unattended. He mumbled something about "liability".

I sat on the edge of the dock, with my feet in the water, discouraged. I knew I was running out of time to find a place to stash my gear and a nice place to bring Cora. I was trying to make the best impression possible, but I was starting to lose hope. I was inclined to think the Isle of Capri would not provide, and began prepping my board to move on down the river when I heard a voice, "Where are you headed on that thing?"

Unknown to me at the time, a couple having a drink under

a large umbrella overheard my conversation with the bartender and were determined to help me find a solution.

"To the Gulf," I smiled into the sun, squinting to see where the voice was coming from.

Jim and Barb were an older couple, wearing smiles and Hawaiian shirts while sipping on fruity drinks as if they were nowhere near Iowa, but on some tropical island in the South Pacific.

"You're going where?!" Jim laughed.

"I almost died a year ago. To celebrate my first year off the life support machines, I've decided to paddleboard the Mississippi River."

"Why?" Barb said, shaking her head with her hand on her cheek. "Your poor mother."

"Well, I rehabilitated on a paddleboard, and I wanted to use it to help raise money for the hospital that kept me alive.

Seemed like a good idea a thousand miles ago." "You call your mother every day, right?" Barb asked.

"Of course!" I lied.

I was so focused on what I needed to accomplish, my mind drifted from our conversation for a minute until Barb spoke again.

"Was it a car accident?"

"Was what a car accident?"

"The reason you almost died?"

"Oh... no, not a car accident." I turned my head and stared out across the river. Sometimes it is easy to tell the story. Other times, it's like trying to describe a homicide. "It was much worse."

Jim changed the subject. "Where are you staying tonight?"

I explained the situation. I told them of Cora and my mission to hitchhike to Cedar Rapids to meet her for the first time.

"Hey, Jeff, come over here." Jim called across the dock.

Enter my river Merlin, Jeff. Magical conjurer of epic solutions. A large man walked up—barrel chested, baldheaded and with big bear hands. He crushed my hand when he shook it. Jeff's friends told him what I was doing and what I needed. Without hesitation, Jeff came to my rescue. Not only did he have a boat docked at the marina where I could stash my board, but he had a BIG boat, a forty-foot cabin cruiser, that would hold me, my gear, and all my new friends. He told me to leave my stuff, go pick up Cora at the airport, and we could all party on his boat for the next few days, free of charge. "Hell, I'm not using it," he said, chew tucked in his lip with a not quite Southern, drawl. "Might as well let someone have fun on it."

He led me to the slip where his boat was docked and gave me the grand tour. I stashed my gear onboard and told him I didn't want to stink when I met my friend so he walked me over to the dock showers located by the bar. It had been a few days since I bathed. I was afraid I'd have to creep into another backyard and use the hose but the marina had some amazing showers, so I dolled up and came out shaved and shiny. I laid out the only clean outfit I had: some surf trunks with duct tape on the left butt cheek, and my blue Pillsbury Doughboy shirt with the words, *Go Ahead, Poke Me*, across the front and went to bed.

At the golden break of day, I hit the road bound for Cedar Rapids. I called Cora and gave her the good news that we had a place to party for her birthday. She teased me, saying that just because people on the river gave me what I wanted, it didn't mean that she would fall victim to the same charm. But it was never me—it was always them—the people of the river and their enormous generosity.

Cora wasn't excited about the idea of hitchhiking back to the marina. I tried to reassure her. "People are great," I told her. "It will be uneventful."

We hung up and I walked into a gas station near the highway. The clerk gave me a funny look when I asked him for a leftover cardboard box.

"My shanty needs a door," I said. He didn't laugh.

Outside, on the curb, I sipped my coffee and wrote with a marker, CEDAR RAPIDS AIRPORT, across the beer box. I wandered up the on-ramp with my IPod on, and my thumb out. I wasn't on the highway for more than fifteen minutes when a beat up old Buick pulled up in front of me.

RIVER JOURNAL,
AUGUST 14, 2011

Kind words from new friends:

"Meeting you was such a blessing to Tom
and me. Reading your story and seeing
your talent for writing fills us with awe.
i read in one post, a note to your mom,
saying that you felt out of place and
wanted to do something with your life to
honor both of your parents. Why can't you
see that you do not have to prove anything
to anyone, except maybe yourself? you are
a gift to this world and your talent for
communication through the written word
proves it. Thank you for coming onto our
shore and may God bless you always."

-Tom and Cat

14

The Wildman from Tipton

Marty scared the hell out of me the moment I opened the silver, sun-blotched door of his beat-up Buick.

I've hitchhiked quite a few times and loved it. I've ridden with gun-toting grannies, architects, students, and construction workers. I've never had a bad experience or even an uneasy feeling about the people picking me up.

Until Marty.

I stood with the door ajar, weighing my options. Something was off about him. He seemed out of place. I almost declined the offer, but, in lieu of using my brain, I climbed in and shut the door. I've never been accused of being the sharpest dart in the board.

Marty's face looked like it was chiseled from marble, with sharp edges. His blue eyes seared like scorching, blue flames. He was like a life-size GI-Joe doll, with cut biceps and Kung-Fu action grip. Every word he spoke was loud and commanding,

"Where you headed?!" He boomed, his face too close to mine.

"Um... The airport in Cedar Rapids," I stuttered.

"I can take you as far as highway 80. You'll have to find your way from there, but it's not too far." I nodded and...*Zoom!* We were off!

I assume that Marty's adrenaline ran a bit higher than most because he talked a mile a minute. His left thumb would tap at the steering wheel while his right elbow dug into the armrest, and he would lean into me when speaking. As we rolled down the highway, I learned that Marty was an ex-army ranger. He had served for nine years. He wasn't afraid to pick me up, not in the least, and he made it clear that if I were a psycho, he would not hesitate to kill me, and he was not opposed to reminding me every few minutes.

"I'll shoot you if you try anything funny." He said, matter-of-factly.

"Please stop saying that." I muttered while my fingernails dug into the passenger side armrest until my knuckles were snow white.

Every time he stared me down and spoke of shooting me, my butt cheeks would clench and my throat felt like cotton. I thought maybe if I told my story he wouldn't see me as a threat. Although, I really don't think he saw me as a threat, anyway. I think he saw me as potential target practice. In the past, telling my story softened people up and drew them closer to me. I was hoping it would have the same effect on Marty. I wasn't sure if it did, but I gave him the short version and was allowed to live for another few minutes.

I turned my focus on getting to know him. I don't have a lot of skills, but getting to know people seems to be a talent I have acquired over the years. I genuinely love people, I think they can sense it, but Marty wasn't making it easy. He was skeptical. I'd ask questions and he'd give me short, punchy answers. Our conversation was like wading through tar. I'd pause for a few uncomfortable moments and watch the green fields roll by before springing another awkward question on him. I wasn't getting through and I think I was starting to annoy him.

"Why all the questions?" He pierced my blue eyes with his own.

"Um, I just thought I'd get to know the man who was going to shoot me for asking too many questions." Marty smiled.

"You're funny." After that, we were friends.

Marty lived in Tipton, where he cared for his wife and mother. His wife had endured two major brain surgeries. I could tell how deeply he loved her when he spoke. I see the stories in a person's eyes when they tell them. I don't know how, I just do. He spoke of his daughters and the quiet life in Tipton. I asked him what he did but for the life of me, I can't remember. After about thirty minutes on the road, the subject moved to the year-long motorcycle trip I took around the country back in 2008. Marty's eyes lit up, fireblue, once more.

"What time does your girl's flight come in?"

I told him a lie, something like she would be arriving within the next hour, because I was still unsure of his intentions. Marty wanted to take me to his house, feed me some lunch, and show me his motorcycles. I was unsure and hesitant at first, but I have this little quirk that once a path diverts, I must see where it leads. My lie meant that I wouldn't have to be there long, so I agreed.

Marty had to make a quick stop at a friend's house to pick up his gun (a bigger one than the one he had with him) and I started doubting my judgment once more. I've never been this bad at analyzing a person and now I might end up dead in the corn fields of Tipton. Soon after the gun stop, we eased into the driveway of a quaint cottage. The sight of his quaint home on a quiet, little street relaxed me a bit.

I kicked off my flip-flops and followed Marty through his back door into a large, airy country kitchen. "Welcome," his wife beamed, handing me a plate with a grilled cheese sandwich and fresh, sliced tomato. I sat in the living room with Marty, his wife, and his mom eating sandwiches and explaining how I came to be sitting in their living room eating their food. After lunch, Marty elaborated on the real reason he wanted to bring me to his home.

"I want to take you riding." He smiled.

My eyes lit up. By now, I was feeling more comfortable with him. Seeing how he interacted with his family helped considerably. There was something so strikingly endearing, insane and wonderful about this man. I couldn't have made up a better character for a story. I pretended to check my messages and told him that Cora's flight was delayed. It wasn't. The truth all along was that her flight was to arrive at four in the afternoon. Things were different now. I sincerely wanted to hang out with him and learn more about his life.

I followed Marty out the back door towards the garage so he could introduce me to his mistresses. When he lifted the garage door, sunlight flooded the exquisite man cave and shimmered off chrome handlebars and tailpipes. The Harleys were magnificent. The cruiser was a mature temptress—dark-skinned with just the right amount of curves in all the best places. The other was a rocket on two wheels with a tight backside. She could hurt you if you didn't hold on tight enough; a heartbreaker all the way.

My river wardrobe of trunks, flip-flops and smartass shirt was unfit attire for riding, but Marty let me borrow some boots and then pointed to the cruiser.

"You can start on that one," he smiled.

I turned the key, pushed the starter, and the bike rumbled as only a Harley can. I gave Marty the thumbs up, and we pulled out of the driveway and into the land of Tipton. Marty gave no instructions. He simply took off, expecting me to keep up.

Back in 2008, I spent a year on a 2004 Honda Shadow. I

traveled over forty thousand miles, sleeping under bridges, with strangers and in the company of old friends. It remains one of the greatest memories of my life. When I returned, I sold my Black Beauty to move to Costa Rica, which eventually led me into the ICU with lots of horror in between.

It had been well over a year, but the old saying is true: You never forget how to ride a bike. The earth rumbled beneath me, filling me with radiant joy. Thunder between my legs. My eyes watered as I reminisced about the days with Black Beauty, traversing this beautiful country. The people, the places, the poetic roads of New England and the enchanting deserts of the West. Entering grand cities on two wheels. I never realized how much I missed life on a motorcycle. It's quite different than life on a paddleboard.

Our first ride was brief—a five minute tease. I followed Marty into a gas station just a few miles from his house to fill up. I couldn't tell if Marty simply knew everybody in town or if he was just a friendly guy by the way he talked to people. He greeted everyone who came within shouting distance.

He finished filling my bike and then got back on his and started it up.

"Aren't you going to fill up?" I asked.

"Not here."

We hit the road once more and I struggled to keep up, but the more miles I laid to pavement, the more comfortable I began to feel. However, I would never ride like Marty. Not in a thousand years. I figured he got the nickname MillionMPH-Marty, because his adrenaline pumped at that speed, but, obviously, he likes to ride at that speed as well.

We zipped through the back hills, passing farm and field. The road would rise and fall to meet us, and Marty and I took turns leading. We were like a pair of dolphins, riding waves in harmonious union, anticipating each other's moves. It wasn't long before I felt as if I had been riding with Marty my whole life.

After what seemed like a flash in time, we pulled into a tiny airfield. We stopped at a couple of pumps and I watched Marty fill his motorcycle with jet fuel... yes, jet fuel. Then he handed me the keys.

I broke into a sweat and the color must have drained from my face because he started laughing. "You'll be fine," he said.

I took the keys and we traded bikes. I pushed the starter and the earth melted beneath me. Did I saddle a lion? Because the bike roared! Maybe it was a bull because it bucked and kicked and I could barely hang on. Whatever animal was beneath me, it was wild. We soared like eagles through rolling farmlands, and the cornfields in my periphery began to blur into bands of gold. My knuckles were fish-belly white, and my heart skipped with every twist of the throttle. Marty rode his bike with palpable ease as if the road did not exist, and maybe it didn't for him.

That's when the revelation slapped me in the face.

Something felt very "off" about Marty when I first met him. My initial interpretation was that I got in the wrong car with the wrong man. But I was mistaken. Watching him tear at the road, riding his Harley as if it were an extension of his legs, I understood my awkward first impression of him. It was the car. He didn't belong in a car. He belonged on a bike.

After a mind-melting hour, we pulled over by a bridge on an old country road for a rest. We sat in the shade watching the meandering brook. I was still reeling from the massive adrenaline rush; it was dripping from my nose. I was so overwhelmed by the day, and the Wildman of Tipton. Marty brought a piece of me back, a part of my spirit that used to frequent my heart from time to time. The "Wildman" on two wheels that still lived inside of me.

We talked about everything and nothing all at once, and the slate sky rumbled in the distance. There was a quiet pause and then Marty spoke, and what he said—I believe— summed up a huge part of who he was. His demeanor calmed, a serious look washed over his face, and his crystal blue eyes softened. "Matt, I love my wife. I love my family and I fucking love the Lord."

I smiled at the thought of all those condemning Christians who would only see Marty for his appearance and language; never acknowledging his commitment to family and his gracious, giving spirit. You don't need those types, Marty. Jesus loves you too, my friend. You can be sure of that. You were the kind of people he hung out with: flawed and rough around the edges. Honest and real.

I turned my eyes east down a road with no end, and then right, following the broken yellow line towards a similar, infinite destination. We were in the middle of all things, two strangers, now friends, sharing a moment in time, and I knew in my heart that this is what life is all about.

Marty knew I had to be leaving soon so we saddled up and rode home. Cora was on her way and I still had to hitchhike from Marty's house to the airport.

On the way back to his house, Marty made a quick stop to pick up some flowers and a card for his wife for no particular reason. We pulled into the garage and put his hogs to bed. "I'm sorry I can't take you to the airport. I have to get to work."

"That's OK, man." I said. "You've done more than enough."

Marty reached out and took hold of my wrist, opened my hand, and laid the keys to his car in them. "Go pick up your girl, take her back to the river, and then toss the keys on the floorboard. I'll get a ride in tomorrow and pick it up." I stood there silent, staring at him in disbelief.

"Oh, and there is cash under the seats. I always keep some

spare cash in there for my daughter when she takes the car, so, please, take whatever I have."

Before I left, Marty searched his garage for something to give me, a token to remember him by (as if I would ever forget). He found a coin with Saint Christopher, the patron saint of travel, on it and placed it in my hand. I may have hugged him, I don't remember. As I pulled out of the driveway, I saw him waving in the rearview mirror. I drove down the highway smiling like the Cheshire cat. The entire day oozed with such random magnificence that I was sure to burst if I tried to squeeze in another moment. But another moment was already on her way.

ooo

I'm not sure what I remember most because it was all such a beautiful sight.

Maybe it was the cowboy hat or the white, hippy blouse. Maybe it was the cut up Daisy Dukes or the flip-flopping sandals on her little feet or it could have been that brilliant smile and the most captivating almond-shaped eyes I had ever seen. Maybe I was so attracted to her soul after a month on the phone that when she skipped up, luggage in tow, to where I stood, she was more beautiful in the flesh than in my dreams.

Whatever it was, I was happy to see Cora.

I waited for her to drop her bag before giving her a hug. I was careful not to make it one of those creepy hugs that linger for too long; it was our first physical contact, but I'm sure she felt my arms tighten and my hands plant firmly on her lower back.

Then, I stepped aside and revealed her chariot — the old, gray Buick. Her eyes lit up when she saw that I had a car. I opened the door for her and had some birthday gifts waiting for her in the passenger seat. After leaving Marty, I stopped at a store and used my lunch allowance for the day to purchase a purple ring, a chocolate-peanut butter truffle, and a card. As a "thank you" she put on some bright red lipstick, kissed each of my cheeks, and we snapped our first picture together.

As nervous as I was, it calmed me to be near her. I've never spent a month simply on the phone with someone before and to think our first date would be floating down the river was pretty wild. As we rolled down the highway, she talked and I kept glancing at her from the corner of my eye. She kicked off her sandals and tucked her cute little legs under her butt, so she was sitting on her knees, leaning back against the door. Her olive skin, caressed by the sun, glowed bronze like the wheat fields waving in the fading dusk light. She smelled amazing. Every sense was heightened in her presence.

I missed my exit.

I got us back on track and an hour later, we arrived at the marina where I escorted her to the boat we would call home for the next two days. Jeff and the rest of the dock residents were in full-blown party mode, adorned in Polynesian attire, complete with straw skirts and thatched hats. He spread the story to the rest of the group while I was gone, and when they spotted us walking down the ramp, they cheered and waved us over to join in the luau.

Cora's friends, Janice and Diane, arrived shortly after, and we all enjoyed Jeff's robust company for a bit before I took them to his boat so they could doll up for Cora's birthday bash. Earlier that day, I had asked Jeff where we could have some fun in the Quad Cities, and he told me to take the bus across the river to the Rock Island District. "You can get into some trouble over there." He smiled.

While the girls got ready, I researched a couple of places where Cora could have a nice birthday dinner, but my plans took a nosedive. By the time we got over to Rock Island, the only restaurants open within walking distance were Subway and Bennigan's. I felt horrible and feared I would rapidly lose points with her and her friends, but Cora was unpretentious and willing to roll with whatever came our way, it didn't even faze her. She was just happy to be in good company. We chose Bennigan's and she pretended to enjoy her dumpy dinner. The lighthearted, funny conversation made up for the food.

Jeff's advice helped make up for dinner. The District was running a festival called *Ya Maka my Weekend*, a Caribbean themed party with live Reggae music. We spent the night dancing, sipping on fruity drinks, and taking crude pictures.

The party ended and the four of us stumbled back to the marina, laughing, shushing, and shout-whispering down the dock towards Jeff's boat. I gave the girls the main cabin and I took the couch. The shenanigans continued until we giggled ourselves to sleep.

Beginning with my cardboard sign, Marty picking me up and our motorcycle rides through cornfields, and finally Cora... it was a day that left me swimming in sweet dreams.

In the morning, we drove around for an hour, looking for pancakes. During breakfast, I overheard Cora tell Janice and Diane that it was the best birthday she ever had. It made my heart skip two beats.

Mission accomplished.

Before Janice and Diane returned to Chicago, they wanted to see how Cora's inflatable kayak would hold up in the Big Muddy. I was curious too, so I pulled out an air pump Jeff had on the boat and in a matter of minutes, we had an instant kayak. It was unexpectedly bigger than anticipated. It looked more like a huge raft. I lifted it from the dock and placed it in the muddy waters of the Mississippi. That's when Diane looked at Cora and said, "Did you finish your swim classes at the YMCA?" To which

Cora replied, "No. I didn't have time. But, I know how to wade in water now, so I should be OK."

I freaked out. "WHAT?! YOU DON'T KNOW HOW TO SWIM?! HOW ARE YOU GOING TO GO DOWN THIS RIVER?!"

Cora smiled, "I just wanted to be with you, don't worry. It will be OK."

Before I could open my mouth to respond, the three of them started laughing.

Funny girl.

I placed the kayak in the water and we both climbed in. Everything worked just fine and soon we were bidding adieu to Janice and Diane.

Our first day together was smooth sailing, what I remember anyway. I was staring at Cora the whole day, so I would be hard pressed to recall any details about the landscape. I do remember that we found a great park to set up camp, and after dinner, Cora read her first journal entry to me so at least one of us was paying attention.

A bridge over muddled waters.

Riding with Marty. Wildman from Tipton!

Humbled.

RIVER JOURNAL,
AUGUST 19, 2011

My detour friends! Hope civilian life
is treating you well. you are never
far from my thoughts. I learned so
much from you in regards to love,
family, and true friendship. and
let us not forget those amazingly
crafty culinary ideas! I'm so craving
a Dorito taco bag right now! Dave
& Terra, Andy & Casey, Jim & Cat,
Matt & Danielle, Nick & Cora... Peace
and love to you all, my friends...

15

Lock and Dam 16

Cora charged into her first day on the river. We managed to knock off fifteen miles, but in her inflatable kayak, I'm sure it felt like fifty.

It was surreal having her there in the flesh. Developing a friendship with a thousand miles between us was easy. However, aside from some insecurity, I honestly felt like we'd been friends my whole life. I melted into her with ease and she walked through my walls as if they never existed, and maybe they didn't to her. But still there was insecurity, and on our second day of paddling the river, I would confront it.

I didn't know how she felt beyond friendship. There were moments on the phone when we traversed the line between friends and potential lovers, but we had decided that neither of us was at a place where there was room for a relationship. For me, that was beginning to slip away.

Our first night camping on the river, I thought I was pretty slick, picking a spot with no trees to hang her Hennessy hammock. "Darn," I smiled, "and me with this one-man tent." I guess she found it charming because she snuggled up next to me and we talked ourselves to sleep.

Though everything seemed to be merging nicely, there remained a subtle gnawing inside that something was off. I tend to overreact and can be overly sensitive, but since she showed up with that big beautiful smile, something told me she was disappointed with the man in person. I knew I had made an impression on her on the phone and with my letters, but the reality of a person can be a different story.

As we paddled together on our second day, I summoned the courage to have my talk with her. If I wasn't what she expected or if she was sorry for committing to two weeks on the Mississippi, I was going to take her back to the airport and send her home with no hard feelings.

After a few miles, I veered us right, and down a slough (a sluggish side channel off the river) where I could find a place to lay my doubts before her. I stepped off my board onto the muddy bank and pulled her kayak to shore. I'm at a point in life where there is no room for small talk. I say what I mean and speak how I feel so I laid it out for her. Our phone conversations naturally grew more intense over the course of a month. I had feelings for her, strong ones, but I was holding my cards close to my chest. I was still a damaged man and had a long way to go before I reached my journey's end. I told her I noticed a difference in her attitude towards me since our official meeting, not a bad attitude, just more reserved than on the phone. I explained to her that if I were not the man in person that she expected, I would help her safely back to the airport and make sure she got on a plane. There would be no ill will whatsoever. I told her I thought she was an amazing person, inside and out, but I expected nothing from her for coming out to meet me.

"Don't be silly," she smiled, "I'm just shy in person. There is no phone or computer to hide behind. I'm just warming up."

"OK," I said.

That was that. We got back in the water and continued on our way. I paddled quietly next to her as she spoke of different things and I loved her voice. I loved how I felt when I was near her and the closer I got to her, the better it was.

Around high noon, we approached the end of our slough. From a distance, I could see it curve back into the Mississippi and beyond the connection, about a half-mile away, was the ominous concrete wall of Lock and Dam 16, stretching over a thousand feet wide, consuming the blue horizon. I snapped out of my Cora-daze and prepared to make our approach.

The best way to describe the majority of Mississippi River locks and dams is that they are large walls of concrete separated into segments by thick concrete piers. Each segment has a gate that may be open or closed, depending on the river level. At the far end, between dam and shore (some on left side, some on right) is the entrance to the lock. The lock itself is about a hundred feet wide and several hundred yards long, making room for the massive river barges. Preferably, you want to hug the side of the river where the lock entrance is located, but as we came out of the slough and re-entered the main channel, I discovered we were on the wrong side.

I searched the shores to my right for a place to portage through, but nothing appeared passable, so I made the decision to paddle across the river, parallel to the dam, so we could enter the lock. I never second-guessed my decision. Paddling parallel to the dam was never a problem in the past.

Sometimes I had to wait for a river barge to lock through and I would paddle in circles outside the lock, up close to the dam—no worries. As we made our way out of the slough, and across the river, I could feel the difference in volume beneath my paddleboard and realized that this time it may be a problem.

The current pulled us to the center fast... too fast. I didn't let on that I was nervous and encouraged Cora to continue paddling. As we paddled past the midway point, I got a visual of the water flowing into the lock channel. The concrete wall separating the lock opening from the dam diverted the water with terrible force. Unless we approached from several yards up river, the current would never allow us safe passage into the lock. Our approach from the center of the river had already left us below the entrance.

I was starting to panic.

I looked back at Cora paddling her kayak with all she had. She was close to exhaustion. I took a line from her kayak and tied it to the back of my board. I pulled at water with my paddle, using all the strength I could summon. We came back upriver within twenty feet of the lock entrance but the current was simply too much for us. That's when I made the decision to turn around, hoping to get us to the other side so we could plan a new course of action.

We never made it.

There was no going forward and no going back. I could feel the girth of the river roaring beneath my paddleboard as the dam drew near.

100 yards.

The concrete wall grew larger.

75 yards.

My stomach churned and twisted into knots.

50 yards.

The gates were down; we would hit them and spend the next several seconds in the vortex of the river until our lungs popped.

25 yards.

In those last seconds of chaotic paddling, a revelation came to the forefront of my mind. I was falling in love with Cora... and now she was going to die.

I pushed aside any useless thoughts detrimental to our situation and focused. I noticed several chains dangling in each segment of the dam known as "Oh, shit" ropes... no explanation necessary.

"Cora, when you hit the wall, grab hold of the chain and hold on tight." She nodded, confirming that she understood, and then I watched her raft slam hard against the iron gate.

It looked like a castle drawbridge. She had a death grip on the chain and her kayak was still right side up. I breathed a sigh of relief and braced myself as my paddleboard smashed against the gate seconds later. My board flipped over. Before going down into the dark turbulent force of muddy water, I grabbed a chain with both hands. Half my body was in the water. The river pulled at my legs with the force of a thousand desperate hands.

I looked over and watched as Cora's kayak filled with water, but because it was inflatable, it was not sinking. My arms were screaming. My shoulders ached.

Think, stupid, think!

I calmed my nerves and barked specific instructions above the roar of angry water. "Cora, get to your cell phone. Call 911 and tell them we are trapped in the middle of Lock and Dam 16 and have them radio the lock operator." She was so brave. There was no screaming, no panicking. As the Mighty slammed her repeatedly against the dam, she maintained her grip on the rope with one hand, and with the other, fumbled through her bag and retrieved her cell from its waterproof case.

No service.

I spoke to her again. "Please don't be scared by what I'm about to do, but I have to try calling for help." I started shouting at the top of my lungs. My hands were burning. Cora was holding on. She was still alive.

My arms grew weary. I pushed away thoughts of going under

or the force of water pressing me against the gate. What would it feel like to have the brunt of the river, from the headwaters to Lock 16, holding me under water? What would it feel like in those last seconds before inhaling liquid? It would be a slow death, the kind of death I'd have time to think about. How tragic. I survived a year ago only to drown in the Mississippi River. However, nothing I could imagine for myself compared to the agony I felt for snuffing out the precious life of this beautiful woman in peril next to me. I would drown before her. I would leave her alone and frightened. She would know I was dead beneath her. I looked into her eyes and she looked into mine. And then her eyes diverted past me. She started yelling, "Just hold on a little longer, I see a boat coming!" My grip softened but I held tight. I glanced over my shoulder at the approaching salvation.

As the boat slowly backed into the dam, one of the crew members stood at the stern swinging a ski rope, trying to decide whom to throw it to first. She screamed at him to throw it to me. I couldn't believe this woman was putting me first. I shouted at him to throw it to her. Back and forth, back and forth; the poor guy stood swinging his ski rope, confused what to do. Cora yelled, "I'm fine! Throw it to him! He's in the water!"

He threw the rope in my direction. The rope was spot on and landed in the water right in front of me. Before I reached out to grasp hold, a nauseating thought swept over me, *If I let go of this rope, I'm a dead man.*

I gripped the handle with all the strength I had and filled my lungs with air wondering if it would be my last. The boat pulled with such force I feared my shoulders would pop out at any moment. Only the force did not belong to the boat; it was the Mighty, the boat never moved. It sat stationary, bobbing back and forth fighting the current. How deceptive this river was. Judging from the surface, one would never anticipate such undertow.

Water forced itself into my mouth and up my nose. My eyelids were lifting free and water gushed into my eye sockets. My hands slipped free.

My head hit concrete and all went black.

I plunged into the darkness below the Mississippi, thrashing and smashing against solid, soulless surfaces. If the dam was closed, it meant I was most likely pinned against the concrete gate waiting to drown. But I was moving, caught in a current. And then... there was light. I opened my eyes and a warm glow filtered through. I grasped at nothing, struggling to move upwards and the light increased in brightness. I broke through the surface and my lungs cried out for air.

I was on the other side of the dam.

I didn't relish in my survival for more than a second before Cora consumed my thoughts. I pulled myself from the river and clambered up the backside of the dam. Dividing the concrete segments are narrow corridors to the other side. I ran through and saw the rescue boat right where I left them.

They looked up at me and shook their heads. My heart sank.

"She went under!" they yelled.

I rushed back just as Cora's head surfaced on the other side. She struggled in the driftwood and trash before finding the concrete ledge behind the gate. I could see the bulging bewildered whites of her eyes as she drew in gulps of air.

Dave, one of the lock operators, called down and ordered me to stay put while they fired the crane and lowered the bucket. I may have heard him, but I wasn't listening. I was already latched onto the face of the dam traversing my way down to her. I didn't know how safe she was. I didn't know if she had a good hold, and there was no way she was going under without a fight. I was not letting her go.

By the time I reached her, the bucket was down, and Dave

was shouting at us to get in. I shoved Cora over the rail and leapt in after her. The crane began to lift us to safety. As the bucket ascended, I pulled her close and held her tight. When we reached the top of the dam, Dave (picture a burly biker who resembles Santa Claus) gave us a bear hug. He had tears in his eyes. "People don't live through that."

As we walked across the top of the dam towards the lock station, I asked Cora what had happened to her.

"After you disappeared, I started to freak out and almost jumped in after you. They had thrown me the rope, but I knew I was going to go under. I thought you were beneath me drowning. I remember holding the rope just as they were about to pull me, I heard your voice yelling on the other side, I took a deep breath and that's when my kayak flipped over. I just remember seeing green water and then darkness as I was carried deep under the dam. I lifted up my hand and I could feel slimy concrete above me. I felt this was my ending and I was going to be trapped under the dam pushed up against a gate. I said a quick prayer and accepted my fate. The next thing I knew, I was at the other side. Had I not heard your voice, I would've never gulped in that extra air to make it."

The crew escorted us to the break room inside the lock station so we could assist with the accident report. They were so kind and tried to make us as comfortable as possible. A couple of them opened the dam so our gear could flow through. They took the boat and gathered all they could find. We could not believe that the only things lost were our flip-flops and Cora's straw cowboy hat. Shame, she loved that hat.

During this time, we learned some things from the crew as I explained to them the reasons behind my river adventure. First fun fact: It was extraordinary that they even spotted us. It was a weekday, and the lock should have been crowded with commercial traffic, directing everyone's attention away from us. The second, and most disturbing fact, was how fortunate we were that the lock was open enough for us to slip through to the other side. The gates should have been closed which would have left us pinned in the pit. The alternative? The gates would have been open just enough to let water through but not enough for a human body which would have left us wedged under the concrete gate.

The guys left us in the break room to chew on the "what ifs" so they could finish all their paperwork. We couldn't sit still and paced about as the reality sank in. Adrenalin subsided and was replaced with anxiety. I couldn't believe I had almost lost her. I imagined calling her parents, telling them their daughter was dead and that it was my fault. Cora went to the bathroom as I continued to pace the floor. Moments snapped and popped as more questions invaded my thoughts. How did this happen? What did I do wrong? Was she actually willing to die for me? Cora returned, and our eyes met. I walked up to her, pulled her close and kissed her.

When the crew was finished with us, my thoughts were diverted to the question, "What now?" I wanted to go home, but I said nothing to Cora. I had almost died a year ago; was it worth losing my life to this river? Even worse, what if Cora had perished under the muddy waters and I had lived? It left me feeling physically sick. I decided the best thing to do would be to get a room in Muscatine and chill out for a couple of days. That's when I would tell her my trip was over.

We said our goodbyes to the crew that saved our lives. Dan was kind enough to offer us a ride to a nearby hotel. We made a stop at Wal-Mart so we could shop in our bare feet for new flip-flops. We looked like a pair of sewer mice walking through the store.

Our hotel was next to Wal-Mart, so we waved goodbye to Dan and I checked us into our room. The manager was very accommodating. The staff dried all our clothes in their commercial dryer and provided us with an armful of towels. We laid out all the towels on our hotel floor and started to unpack everything to lay them out to dry. That's when I broke the news.

"It's over. We're going home."

I was sitting in the chair by the window and she was on the floor with her backpack between her knees. She started to cry. Through a flurry of sobs and scolding, she told me that she believed in my progress with all of her heart. She believed I had survived the hospital for a reason, that this quest would be life-changing for others as well as myself and she would not be to blame for me quitting. "If only you knew how I feel about this journey, you would have more faith. I did not fly all the way out here just for you to quit because of me. We should get right back on that river instead of staying in this hotel and not let your fears get the best of us!"

I struggled to find more excuses. I looked around the room at all of our waterlogged possessions. I grabbed my backpack from the floor that held my computer; it was my prized possession and it contained hours of writings about my journey, the people I had met, and my experiences. I had blogged and written chapters in preparation for this book—thousands of words and a heap of letters and journals. They were gone now.

"Cora, the book is gone... every word, and I don't have the will to start over."

She would not back down. "Open it."

With a sigh, I placed it on the bed. I stored my computer in three different dry bags, one larger than the next. I opened the first... my wallet and all of my maps were swimming in a heap of water. I opened the second and more water poured out along with wet energy bars. I gave Cora a look as if to say, "See," and she shot me one back that said, "Continue!" I opened up the third and last sack, and it was evidence enough for me when I reached in and felt the water pooled at the bottom. I pulled out my Ipod and turned it on... dead. I pulled out Cora's mini radio and turned it on... dead. I pulled out my cellphone and turned it on... dead. All had no power light of life. I shook my head. "This computer is done."

I set the laptop on the bed, tossed the bag aside and noticed the computer was dry... not a single drop. I flipped up the lid and found nothing but bone-dry keys. I looked at Cora, my face painted with disbelief. "This isn't possible." I turned it on and the screen glowed to life and there was my book, staring me in the face.

Cora smiled at me.

"Ok." I said. "I won't give up."

RIVER JOURNAL,
AUGUST 22, 2011

I'm so very happy that I don't have
to call Cora's parents and tell them
i drowned their daughter her second
day on the river. To the men of lock
and dam 16: Words will never do
justice the gratitude I feel for you.
Thank you for saving our lives.

16

Onward and Southward

The dam experience anchored me to Cora in a way that helped me understand something my heart already knew: I had been falling in love with her for a month while talking for hours on the phone until my exhausted body could not stay awake for another word.

It happened slowly at first, then slapped me in the face when I wasn't looking.

We set sail for St. Louis. I had eight more days before she would leave me to the river. It was a lofty goal—I knew the river and my physical restrictions—but Cora was motivated. I had told her there might be days where the pain was so great I couldn't get out of bed. It was difficult to share myself in such ways. To be completely vulnerable and exposed.

Her response: "Then I'll lie next to you until your pain goes away."

Cora flew into Cedar Rapids on August 13. After a Quad City birthday celebration and a thrill ride through the dam, she was already six days into her fourteen-day trip. No way were we reaching St. Louis before she was to fly out on August 26, but our destination didn't matter to me. I drank in every second with her like a desert cactus collecting rain. I was still in awe that she was so willing to continue on the river. What kind of person would fly a thousand miles to be with a man she's never met, almost drown on their second day together, and then get back in the water? I wanted her to have a good time more than anything else. I wanted her to remember me. I wanted a place in her heart that any other adventure that followed could not replace.

We spent two days in Muscatine recuperating. I was less than eager to get back on the river, but after the computer phenomenon and Cora's devotion to my story, I pulled up my big-boy pants and prepared to paddle. After a time of binge eating and a few bottles of wine, there was no more stalling. We just had to figure out how to get our gear back to the river. There was a Ford dealership next to our hotel, so we went in to see if somebody there could offer us a ride. We explained our predicament, and a man came to our aid. He offered to load us up in one of their rental trucks. He dropped us off at Riverside Park and snapped a photo with us. Everyone wanted a token of the loonies on the Mighty. We thanked him, said goodbye and I went into river mode, carefully packing her kayak and my paddleboard.

At first, I simply didn't notice what peered down on us from upriver. Cora was busy applying sunblock when I touched the small of her back and pointed upstream at the ominous concrete structure. It stretched across the Mighty, glowing in the morning sunlight, popping grays and pinks off a blue jay backdrop. It looked like something out of a Star Wars movie. We stood together staring at the backside of Lock and Dam 16, attempting to ignore the memories of gushing water and cries of desperation. Deciding the view offered no benefit to the day's paddle, we turned our backs, boarded our vessels, and allowed the "almost" and "what ifs" to disappear quietly around the next river bend.

Cora brought a plastic water case for her cellphone that managed to survive the dam. When her service picked up satellite, we enjoyed Pandora while floating side by side, laughing and scheming of days to come. That was the day John Mayer's, *Edge of Desire*, became our song.

All men have seen beautiful women. From the moment a straight young boy realizes what a beautiful woman is, it is the beginning of a lifelong pursuit to see more beautiful women. I've seen many throughout my life. I've seen them at the beach, on mountains, hiking through forests, riding subways, and strolling past me in almost every state in the continental US. I can say with all passion and honesty— none made me feel the way I did when I looked at Cora, floating next to me on a muddy river, her tanned skin shimmering under a canopy of golden sunlight. When she grew weary, she would stretch her arms, arching her perfect form towards the heavens and I would lose balance every time. I wanted to live on that river, watching her stretch and smile, for the rest of my life.

Our first day after the dam was a success, in the sense that there were no life-threatening perils, simply a gentle paddle with lots of laughter and stolen kisses. We were back in the flow of lazy hours, watching green landscapes roll into little river towns.

By late afternoon, we landed in New Boston and pitched our tent beside Dave and Mary, a sweet retired couple who spent their weekends camping out in their RV by the river. Normally, it's not permitted to set up a tent without payment or being a resident of the park, but Dave welcomed us in. "You'll be our guests for the evening. If anyone asks, tell them you're with us."

We asked about dinner options and Dave pointed us in the direction of the only place within walking distance. Mary was hesitant; said it was the type of establishment that could get "a little rough."

She was right. We weren't in the bar two minutes before the men were making passes at Cora right in front of me. The looks didn't bother me so much; you can't be with an attractive woman and expect people to not look at her, that type of insecurity is a young man's game. Disrespecting her in front of me was a whole other level of trouble. It didn't take me long to notice that she was the only woman in a bar full of roughnecks. Even the owner came over and squeezed up close to her. Cora was beyond uncomfortable and they could smell it. It made them more aggressive. I inconspicuously gripped the saltshaker in my hand; if someone put a hand on her, I was going to punch it into their eye socket. Cora could tell by my demeanor that I'd had enough. She complained about being nauseated to give me an opening. Nobody had asked to take our order, so I took her by the arm and got the hell out.

We were still hungry when we returned to the campsite, so Dave took us up to a convenience store in his golf cart. We spent the evening chatting by the fire outside their RV and they spoke of their children and life up north. It was the part of my journey I wanted Cora to experience the most—the people.

The next morning, Mary stocked us up with some fruit and homemade jalapeno venison jerky. We said our goodbyes and set out for Burlington. If we were to reach our goal by nightfall, we would need to paddle over thirty-five miles. It would be our longest paddle together.

After a full day of uneventful paddling, we floated beneath the bridge welcoming us into Burlington just as the sun fell behind the midwestern hillside. As we paddled towards the dock, two pontoon boats approached before we could reach the marina. Both families aboard had read about me in the paper. After a few minutes asking questions about my journey, they invited us to climb up and join them for dinner and a dry place to sleep. I protested, stating that we would be happy in our tent, but they all insisted that there was nowhere to camp. We felt conflicted, not wanting to offend, until one of them mentioned that their cabin did not have running water. With that, we thanked them for their offer and climbed onto the other boat.

The chosen pontoon pulled up to shore on the east bank where two RVs nestled into the woods by the water's edge. We exited the boat and carried our gear towards the smaller of the two RVs, as instructed.

They were a nice family that included a burley middle-aged man, his wife, his grandchild, and his mother. They offered us their shower in the big RV while they grilled up some steak. Feeling fresh and clean, we sat down to enjoy our homemade dinner. Oddly enough, we were the only ones eating. The family just sat and watched. When we finished, the woman gathered our dishes and left us to enjoy the crackling fire. That's when I noticed the baby on grandpas' lap was slurping on something in a koozie. Come to discover, Grandpa was sharing his can of beer with his twoyear-old grandson. He caught us looking, shot us a devilish grin, and gestured with his finger for us to keep quiet.

As the night progressed, the drinking accelerated, and the man became increasingly obnoxious and crude towards Cora. What was she to do but laugh politely after each innuendo and elbow poke he gave her? She shot me the look as if to say, "Let's go to bed... NOW!" We thanked them for dinner and politely excused ourselves so we could cuddle up in the hot RV away from his obnoxiousness. Cora was anxious and sleep was sporadic with every clink and clatter that came in the night. Eventually, we fell into deep sleep only to be awakened once more by violent vibrations and clanking chains.

The RV was moving.

In a panic, Cora leapt for the nearest window and threw back the curtains while I tried to open the door. "It's locked!" I yelled. Cora was frantic so I pulled her close and held her tight. The RV flew down the rocky road like a bat outta hell! It made a sharp right; I lost my grip, and had to watch helplessly as she bounced off the wall. I was still in a post-sleep, drowsy stupor but continued searching for a way to escape. No luck. Our only door was locked and the window wasn't big enough for us to crawl through. Then it hit me. The roof vent. I climbed on the bed and starting cranking the hatch, but the handle broke off in my hand, so I used my back as a battering ram. After three bone rattling slams, I broke through. I climbed up and then dropped to my stomach and lowered my arm to Cora's outstretched hands and we soon found ourselves on top of the moving RV. I grabbed hold of her trembling hand and without hesitation; we jumped off the RV into darkness.

Then I woke up. Just a bad dream.

A pale light crept slowly through the grimy windows signaling that dawn was in tow. I was in so much pain and knew that I could not paddle without some more rest, so we made plans to cross the river to Burlington and nap at the park near the boat ramp.

Of course they weren't going to kidnap us in their RV, it was just a crazy dream, but the raunchy comments to Cora the night before and the beer-gulping baby was enough for me to realize that I needed to be more careful about where I allowed my paddling partner to sleep at night.

Cora and I reached the Burlington public boat ramp in forty-five minutes, and pulled our gear up the concrete slip. After securing our gear, we set our sights on breakfast. As we hiked up the main road, an elderly man with a gentle smile pulled up beside us and offered us a ride to a local café. "I highly recommend it!" he said. We extended him an invitation to join us but he kindly declined.

After a satisfying meal at Jerry's Main Lunch, we started walking back to the ramp when the same nice man drove up and offered us another ride. "I thought maybe you'd be done about now."

We climbed in and on the way back, he gave us a tour of the town. We learned that Burlington suffered a massive fire after a lunatic decided to light up a church. It was also home to the country's longest, winding road, beating out San Francisco's famous Lombard Road. After the tour, the kind old man dropped us off at the boat ramp and Cora spread out a blanket in the grass so we could nap. Throughout the morning, cars backed their boats into the water without problem or complaint that our gear was tucked away off to the side. That is, until the little red tugboat arrived.

I roused from my nap to the rumbling sounds of a dually backing down the ramp with a homemade tugboat in tow. I noticed him struggling to keep it straight, shaking his head and mouthing angrily into the rearview mirror.

"Cora, look at this guy. Is he shouting at us?" I asked.

"Why would he? Our stuff isn't in his way," She replied.

That's when a tall, lanky man with black hair and a thick mustache jumped gruffly out of the car, slamming his door. He yelled, "Somebody get this shit out of my way!"

It was not a good morning for me. I didn't want Cora to see my temper, but there was something about this guy that was causing me to boil. I called over to him. "Is there a problem? That's our stuff. It's been there all morning with no complaints from the other boaters. Why are you having such a hard time?"

The man's scrawny face with his wiry out-of-place mustache

looked up to where we lay on our blanket. "Move your stuff or I'll move it for you!" He stomped over to Cora's blue kayak.

The day before, Cora's inflatable kayak suffered a small puncture on the bottom, possibly from pulling it to shore on one of our breaks. I had some extra-sticky duct tape that seemed to be holding it just fine but dragging it across the concrete boat ramp would not be a good thing and that's exactly what he did.

Mustache guy snatched Cora's kayak in one hand and my paddleboard in the other and pulled, scraping them both across the cement. I sprinted from our blanket to where he stood twenty yards away and shoved him with the force of a sledgehammer. I don't think it was the reaction he expected because his eyes bulged out as he stumbled back, struggling to find balance. "Touch it again, I dare you." I said calmly.

He took a half-step and leaned towards our equipment once more when I was on him with another shove. He stumbled back several steps and slammed against the wooden dock flanking the boat ramp. He scrambled to climb the dock before I could attack a third time. But I wasn't finished getting my point across. The man turned to face me as he backpedaled, threatening to call the police if I hit him, but I didn't hear what he said. I wanted him to swing at me, and I gave him the chance by slamming my palms into his chest a third time, pushing him further away from our gear. Cora jumped up on the dock and stood between us with her hands on my chest, speaking calmly and soothingly, asking that I not hit the man.

"Yeah, good thing your girlfriend came to your rescue."

She glared at him, "I just saved you from a bad day!"

I knew he wasn't worth it nor was he going to put up a fight. He just wanted to aggravate. Completely frustrated, I surrendered to Cora's request and jumped off the dock in a squalling rampage and the man scurried to his truck to call the police. People stood by watching in disbelief and I suddenly became aware that I was a stranger in their land. As I crossed the boat ramp towards our gear, I noticed a dead catfish with a missing eye floating in the oily water. I picked up the carcass and hurled it at Mustache guy. It somersaulted through the air and landed at his feet.

Cora met me back at the blanket where I patiently waited for the police to arrive. I figured the witnesses would call me the aggressor and I would probably be going to jail.

I soon found myself surrounded by two police officers. I explained our side of the story and how mustache guy was jeopardizing our only mode of transportation down the river. All morning, other boats backed in and out with no problems until he showed up. They informed me that he was fearful for his life and I laughed, pointing out the fact that he was bigger than I was. They also questioned the bystanders who watched the whole thing. In the end, the police concluded that I wasn't at fault according to witnesses. I apologized to them for the disturbance and promised to be on my way. The officers were very nice and one of them stood talking to me for another few minutes about my adventure down the river.

As we were packing up, Cora started laughing at the thought of me throwing the dead fish. "You're crazy! What possessed you to pick up a fish and throw it at him?"

"You interrupted me and I still had some pent-up aggression." I smiled.

Throughout the shove match and our interview with the police, an elderly couple had been watching from the front seat of their Ford F-150. After the cops left and we began prepping our gear for launch, they pulled up beside us and rolled down the window. Knowing this was not my town, I was expecting the locals to force us out of Burlington, but was pleasantly surprised when he stuck his head out and said with a grin, "I would have hit him." Gotta love the Midwest!

There would be no rest in Burlington so we set course for Fort Madison, followed by Montrose, Keokuk, and then on to Quincy. I didn't say it, but I was quite certain that Quincy would be as far as we would paddle together before she left me to the Mighty. I hoped for Hannibal, so we could spend some time together in the childhood home of Mark Twain. Worst case, we would get to Quincy, rent a car, spend the morning in Hannibal, and then I would take her to the airport in St. Louis.

It used to be that days were like weeks on the river. Now they were fleeting. Every hour spent gazing at her in the sunlight, singing along to the music on her phone, and enjoying endless conversations, sank from time as quick as a rock in the river. We talked and shared our dreams beyond the river. She would speak of a future that included me and my heart would swell. I tried to keep my cards close to my chest. I knew I had a long way to go and I know what distance and time does to people. Especially those whose only investment is a little phone talk and a two-week river adventure. We did have the dam, though. That could solidify her to me, but that was nothing more than a traumatic experience and those are unreliable at best. I knew how I felt about her, but in my heart, I conceded to the fact that I would probably be nothing more than another notch on her life experience belt. What future could I offer? I was a poor aspiring author who lived on the road and wanted nothing to do with conventional life. I was certain that the moment her plane landed in Orlando, she would re-enter her own reality and the lonely river rat she shared time with would begin to slip from the front of her mind. With enough time, I would be nothing more than a sweet memory. It had to be that way.

I enjoyed those passing seconds to the fullest. We would

explore dilapidated river cabins and lonely islands during our daily paddle. By night, we would hunt down some hot food and a cold margarita before snuggling up in my one-person tent. Thoughts would seep into my head that this adventure was not supposed to be so comfortable. It was a duel between man and nature, but that was ridiculous. I battled more nature a year ago than most do in a lifetime when my organs failed and my body began to bleed out. I battled nature from the first wiggle of my toe, to dropping my walker six months later. Nature gave me a beating that first day of the river and it continued to pound me every day since with slow currents and strong headwinds. I'd battled enough. I was going to enjoy the fruits of life that were graced upon me in the form of this beautiful, spontaneous, caring woman who brought stillness to my soul.

Side by side, we paddled the Muddy, leaving Burlington in our past. For miles, there was nothing but scorching rays, waving boaters and small islands. No towns, no place to take a break. Then, in the early afternoon, I noticed boaters gathering on a sandbar about a half a mile ahead of us. Nice! I was going to have the pleasure of introducing Cora to one of my favorite pastimes on the Mighty Miss—sandbar parties. Even on weekdays, people were out partying on the river. On our approach, we caught the attention of a couple who were enjoying the afternoon with their two young children. They offered us some watermelon and we sat in the water by their boat and talked about our trip while their kids played on my SUP.

After our break, it was back to the river. An exhausting few hours lay ahead of us with the hot sun beating down. The rest of the day was uneventful and before we knew it, the light was beginning to dim as we approached the bridge, ushering us into Fort Madison.

On our fifth day together, the nature battle continued

after Fort Madison with more fierce head winds. The worst I'd encountered. I noticed on my map that there was a bloated elbow, curving left, just above Montrose. We could see the town far off, but seeing a town is almost worse than not seeing one at all, because they sit perched in the distance and what you think is no more than an hour away is actually more like four. As it was with the bridge at Fort Madison the night before, the visual distance can be very deceiving.

The elbow in the river was just that—an elbow in the face with every pull of my paddle. I began to wonder if the current was flowing in the opposite direction. To our right was a dense field of reeds and lily pads. To the left, Nauvoo, Illinois. I entertained the thought of crossing but it was over a mile from our position. We needed rest, but it would be the lesser of two evils to push forward to Montrose. For another hour, we fought for a mile. I couldn't stand to watch Cora struggle in that awful kayak. I hooked her up to my paddleboard and towed her for a bit so she could rest. The poor woman inched that inflatable blue corpse through the water for more miles than I would have. She packed considerably light, but it was still too much for the kayak. I was guilty of the same thing on my first day. It's hard to leave a world of comfort and enter a land of nothing.

As we sank below the elbow, the headwinds blew so savagely that each time I raised my paddle for another stroke, I would lose the inches I just paddled. I grew frustrated and cursed with winds. Cora kept sending flirty comments my way about how nice my back looked when I was paddling, and I struggled to maintain my ego even though I wanted to drop to my knees and beg for mercy. It angered me that I was powerless to the pain my diseases inflicted upon me. Cora tried everything. She pulled out her phone and used the internet to research Nauvoo. She started reading me the history of the town, hoping that it would take my mind off the malicious headwinds.

"Did you know Nauvoo used to be called Commerce before Joseph Smith, founder of the Latter-Day Saints, renamed it in 1839?"

"Uh-huh." *Pant... Pant... Wheeze*

"A large village of Sauk and Meskwaki Indians lived nearby Nauvoo in the 18th century." "That's cool." *Holy crap, I'm tired.*

"This isn't helping is it?"

I stopped paddling, looked back at her and smiled. "Not really, but I like the sound of your voice."

After hours of headwind torture, we hit solid ground and docked at the quiet town of Montrose. There was a park at the river's edge. We tied up our gear and I collapsed in the soft evergreen grass that separated the town from the Mississippi. Cora laid out a blanket and I took a long nap under the shade trees. I'm not sure how long I slept, but I could have stayed there forever. When I awoke, Cora had already scouted out a quaint little sports bar just over the railroad tracks, so we stashed our gear and went in to get a bite.

After an early dinner, Cora wanted to paddle on to Keokuk, but I was done. We knew it was our next big town and she was hoping to get a hotel room with a hot shower and a comfortable bed, so I could get a couple days rest. She could sense my pain. The paddle against the headwinds left me thoroughly spent and aching. I just wanted to make camp right there in the park. Thankfully, during dinner, the owner of the bar called the mayor (you know you're in a small town when the mayor is on speed-dial) and we had permission to do just that. Cora relented but not without protest. She really didn't want me sleeping on the hard ground another night.

As we began dragging our gear from the water, Tom and

Kathy Richardson strolled up the rickety old dock to board their pontoon boat with their friends. They were in Montrose for dinner and were about to head back to their riverfront home in Keokuk when Tom turned and asked what the crazy contraption was floating in the water next to his boat. I was in so much pain that it was a chore just to tell my story. Cora could tell and she took point and explained what my paddleboard was and what I was doing. When she was done, Tom and Kathy invited us to enjoy a hot shower and warm bed for the evening.

It may start to sound as if all I did was scout out people to use for food and shelter, but nothing could be farther from the truth. The people I stayed with represented a fraction of my nights on the river. I actually preferred to camp. Reason being: I was dealing with an affliction that caused my joints to burn like scorching blue flames. Camping allowed me to move at my own pace or sleep in all morning. When people invited me over, I felt it was rude if I didn't wake up when they did and hit the water, no matter how much I hurt. Not that anyone ever made me feel that way, most folks invited me to stay longer. It was just my upbringing, I guess. Accepting the kindness of strangers, and giving nothing in return was very difficult. I didn't believe I deserved it, but the kindness never stopped. I'd refuse and they would insist. They wanted their friends, their kids and their neighbors to hear the story of my miracle. The most popular reason people gave me on the river for inviting me in was that they wanted to feel like they were a part of the adventure and it made me happy to give that to them-if only for a night.

I think so many of the people we met were drawn to us because they had children of their own, scattered across the country, and it made their parental hearts ache for the lonely couple sleeping in a tent. Snuggled up to Cora in a tiny tent was nothing short of bliss for me, but I wanted her to be as comfortable as possible, so when the lovely Richardsons offered, I happily obliged.

We spent a wonderful evening in the warm comfort of Tom and Kathy's beautiful riverside home. I shared my story and adventure with them and some of their friends. Kathy treated us to some crackers and various cheeses while Tom and I sipped on a glass or two of Gentlemen Jack. Tom warned me that the next stretch of the river was prone to treacherous headwinds and offered to pick us up above Lock and Dam 18 and deliver us safely to the other side. This was a delightful song to Cora. After almost drowning at number sixteen, she actually had the courage to pass through number seventeen. We slipped through without incident and snapped a happy selfie while the lock dropped, but an opportunity to avoid the next dam was music to her.

In the morning, we said our goodbyes to Tom and Kathy and were right back on the river treadmill. I wasn't fully recovered from the day before. Typically, I would have spent the day lying in my tent popping pain pills, but I didn't want to abuse the Richardson's hospitality. They would have let us stay for a week if needed.

By noon, my body had quit on me again. Tom was right. The section of river north of Lock and Dam 18 was torturous. I simply had nothing left to give. We pulled our gear up on an abandoned dock and hiked up the bank to call Tom. He was surprised to hear that we had made it to the dam already. Cora explained to him through the phone that this was not the case.

"Matt's in a lot of pain, Tom."

"I'm on my way."

As if the Richardsons weren't generous enough, Tom knew a kind lady who had connections at the Hampton Inn and arranged for us to have a free room for the night. Tom even set me up to be interviewed at the hotel by the local paper.

Later that night, snuggled up watching TV, Cora looked at me with a curious smile. "What is it about you that is so easy for people to love?"

I smiled back. She talked so sweetly to me. "Honey, it's not that people love me. It's that the world is full of good and beautiful people who simply love, regardless of the person." A truth that was proven to me more times than I have put to pen.

The next morning, I still wasn't ready for the river. I tried to get out of bed and it felt like my joints were coated in hot tar. I was embarrassed to show Cora my frailty, but it was undeniable. The remnants of the incident would have its way with me no matter how tough I tried to act. She didn't bat an eye. She paid for an additional night then went into town and bought snacks, cold drinks, and some Epsom salt so I could soak my pain away. After another day of recuperation, I was ready to SUP.

Tom's kindness continued when he offered to pick us up at the hotel and take us back to the river. He was such a gentle and sweet soul. He reminded me of my father, and even looked at me with the same concern and affection in his eyes as my dad. He stood there, white parted hair glistening in the sun, in his pressed Dockers and button-down shirt, and watched quietly as we strapped our gear down. I knew he didn't want to leave until we were safely around the next bend. Cora hugged him and kissed his cheek. I went in for a handshake but traded it for a hug. I wanted to tell him that he brought a piece of my dad back to the river, but instead we paddled away, leaving him in our wake like all the others who had come to my aid before him. Nevertheless, the memory of his kindness will stay with me forever.

In two days, we would arrive in Quincy and my time with Cora would be over.

RIVER JOURNAL,
AUGUST 28, 2011

Jim Dandy! It's Tumbleweed!
Where does happy live, my
friend? i think many a place
and sight on this river. i can't
thank you enough for the
journey you made to bring me
Miss sunshine. Till we meet
again on sunny dry shores.

17

For Two Weeks I Fell

The sun dripped into the west, casting pale yellows against the iron bridge that spanned the Mississippi, connecting Iowa and Illinois. As we approached Quincy, I was fully aware that my journey with Cora would end once my paddleboard struck mud and we pulled our vessels from the water. It would be the last time I would extend my hand to help her from the kayak. It would be the last time I'd see her stretch towards the heavens, her soft frame finding relief from the day's exertion.

For two weeks I fell, I tried my best not to, but in the end, I had no chance at all. I told myself to keep a safe distance so that the sting would be minimal when she left. I believed she cared for me. We paddled for many hours, side by side, in perfect harmony and sincerely enjoyed each other's company, but I also knew that once a person departs from a unique experienced and is reinserted into the comings and goings of everyday life, they tend to move on. I had more days ahead and plenty of miles to paddle. This was not her journey. It was still mine, alone. With that revelation, the darkness began to make its way back into my heart.

The Bay Bridge grew larger with every draw of my paddle.

I slowed my pace, but the river moved on. How did it go by so fast? When I was alone, each day on the river was like a week; with Cora, each day felt like a minute.

Davenport birthday, Muscatine dam, Burlington fish fight, Fort Madison, Keokuk—together we paddled, built stories and shared memories that I felt confident (because of their uniqueness) had left a permanent impression on her heart. She could not forget me. At least that's what I kept telling myself.

I watched her paddle at my flank. The deeper the sun set, the more her skin glowed. I watched her with soft eyes and wondered how she came to be on this river, floating her days away in my company. Seven billion souls inhabit this great blue planet; out of them all, I found her... and she found me.

We veered left at the bridge and traveled a slough for a hundred yards until we reached the Quincy Boat Club. Patrons of The Pier restaurant looked down at us from their perch behind a wall of glass, pointing and waving. At the boat club, a kind member allowed us to store our gear, promising safety, as we arranged for a place to sleep. He told us the Blues Festival in Washington Park was the place to be on that cool evening so we quickly located a hotel, checked in, and prepared for our last night of fun.

We had a nice dinner and ambled the streets, hand in hand, listening to live music. I resisted the urge to go all "Matt" on her by pulling away and acting as if her absence would be painless. No, I let her know it would hurt, and that I'd miss her with every quiet minute that passed as I paddled the river alone.

We never reached our goal of St. Louis. We wanted to end our journey together at the Gateway Arch, but it was too lofty to begin with. I didn't want to dampen her optimistic spirit, I just understood the reality of how fast I could move on the river. In the end, I was satisfied with our accomplishment and everything we had endured together.

On the day of her departure, we rented a car so I could drive her to the St. Louis airport. A distance that took an hour by car—days by river. Her plane left in the afternoon, so we would realize our plan to spend the morning in Hannibal, the childhood home of Mark Twain, before saying goodbye.

It was a good day. We toured the town and took pictures by Tom Sawyer's famous fence. We pretended the inevitable did not exist and I allowed myself to laugh and smile. Strolling through Hannibal, accompanied by the spirit of Mark Twain, filled me with a sense of accomplishment; I was a true modern day Huckleberry Finn. Being there with Cora, holding her hand, filled me with happiness and I knew, in that moment, my adventure would include a love story.

I did my best to keep her close in those final fleeting seconds. So close, in fact, that she almost missed her plane and had to get out and run with nothing more than a quick kiss before disappearing into a sea of faces.

And once again, I was alone.

I drove back to Quincy in a mixed state of happiness and gratefulness, both simmering inside of a broken heart. Two weeks came and went, and I never told her. I had so much I wanted to say. I wanted her to know that I was captivated from the moment I saw her. I wanted her to know how she lit up my darkness. I wanted her to know that when I was next to her, I was at peace. But most importantly...

I wanted her to know that I loved her. Now she was gone. More than likely, we would continue our phone conversations for a while, but eventually, I was sure to fade from her heart and mind.

The following morning, I prepared for two television news

interviews. Anything to ease my sadness. I would then rest for one more evening before returning to the Mighty. Both interviews were held at the dock where Cora and I finished our journey together. During my second interview, I noticed a sizable group of people, upriver, gathered at the dock.

"It's a search party," the reporter said. "Two people drowned in a boat accident yesterday and they are searching the back slough for the bodies."

After the interview, I thanked the reporter, and then I hopped on my SUP and paddled up the channel until I reached the cluster of boats that made up the search party. I wanted to offer my services, knowing I could paddle the narrow back channels where boats couldn't fit. A friend of one of the lost shook my hand, and with damp eyes said, "Thank you. We'd appreciate having you."

I spent the better part of an afternoon squeezing through side sloughs, ducking under trees while dipping my paddle into the water towards anything that resembled a body. It reminded me of northern Minnesota where the river was so shallow and narrow, I'd have to jump off my SUP and drag it through the mud. Sometimes, I'd approach fallen trees, or places where the current was obstructed, and would see pale colored objects wedged against them under the surface. My heart would skip a beat as I drew closer, only to discover that it was a milk jug or some other obscure piece of trash glowing against the sunlight.

I prayed I would find the bodies so that the families involved could have closure. But I also wanted to vomit at the thought. I stayed vigilant until the sun dropped behind the Bay Bridge. No bodies were found that day.

That evening, I ordered a pizza and retired to my room so I could begin preparations for the morning's departure. I needed rest, but sleep eluded me. Truth be told, it was one of my most difficult nights on the river. The thought of waking up and entering the waters alone made my heart ache and threatened to steal my resolve. Deep in my depths, however, I knew that allowing Cora into my life was the best thing for me, no matter the duration. No matter the outcome. The story of Cora, the very existence of Cora-I could not imagine a better addition to my journey.

We can hide our hearts if that's what is needed for survival. I often do and cannot pass judgment on others for something I do myself. I can only talk from experience. I don't know a lot of things, but I can explain to a person what it's like to almost die. I can describe the panic inducing sounds of an ICU and the unique smell accompanying death. I can also tell of beautiful things. I can tell what the roads cutting through Anytown, USA, smells like on two wheels. I can describe the twists and turns of a Mighty river. But one thing I'll never be able to explain, despite my futile attempts, is why human beings can be surrounded by so many, yet feel so alone.

There's no denying that we long for closeness, but not too close, so we put up walls, allowing people to enter the outer court, but no further, knowing full well this will never amount to any sort of substantial relationship. And the cycle continues. Why is it the philosophy of a broken heart to shut down, denying love another shot? Perhaps the same reason a hand recoils from a hot stove. It remembers the burn.

Lazy philosophies no longer mattered. I could not betray my heart. I was in love with Cora. She brought life back into my broken heart.

So what did I do?

That night, alone in my hotel room, I drank a bottle of Jack Daniels and wrote her an email telling her to move on and not to play with fire.

RIVER JOURNAL,
SEPTEMBER 6, 2011

Today, i met a young woman named
darla. she lost her parents to Hurricane
katrina and has been piecing her heart
back together ever since. i tried to extract
her story without being too obtrusive, but
she was reluctant. That's ok. i love sharing
stories but they should flow naturally like
the river. either way, darla is a reminder
that somebody always has it worse... and
there is a sad sense of encouragement in
that. sad because somebody has it worse
and they are hurting. encouraging because
it reminds me how truly blessed i am. it's
also a reminder that people are like books.
They should not be judged by their current
chapter, but by their complete story. our lives
move through seasons. be sensitive to one
another.

18

BJ and The Bear

The distance between river towns continued to spread after Hannibal. It took me a day from Hannibal to reach the town of Louisiana. Alton would be the next substantial river town before my midway point in St. Louis. I was not prepared for the Louisiana/Alton stretch of the river but it was a good education as to what I could expect from the lower Mississippi in terms of basic needs for survival. If I didn't have enough water or supplies, then it would be tough luck. Plan better next time.

My parents were meeting me in St. Louis, so I was at full throttle. I had to reach Alton if I were to make it to the great Arch the following evening. The last thing I wanted to do was fall behind, forcing them to drive north to intercept me. I just wanted to make St. Louis, put my paddleboard aside for a few days and rest. There had been many hot days on the river, but I remember the stretch from Louisiana to St. Louis as some of the worst. I awoke knowing that I was late getting on the river by the scorching vapors in my tent. Anxious to reach my goal, I decided against searching for water at breakfast and made due with the half a jug I had from the day before. I left Louisiana for Alton, and by noon, I was completely out of water.

By midafternoon, I approached Lock and Dam 25 famished with a mouth full of cotton. It happened only twice before that I wasn't allowed to lock through a dam. Why shouldn't my third denial be on a day where I was feeling faint with thirst and had no available liquids for miles? To make things even more magical, Lock and Dam 25 had a solid rock incline that rose fifty feet above the surface of the river. I had no shore to portage on—just rocks—big ones. I pulled over and sat on what I thought to be the most comfortable boulder, anchored my SUP with my foot and started untying my packs. It wasn't possible to carry everything up the rocks in one trip, so I hoisted my gear in stages, starting with the paddleboard. I carried (more like dragged) Miss Sunshine to the top, then traversed back down in reverse for each of my packs. Three trips later, I was beyond thirsty and I still needed to hike to the other side of the lock. When walking the length of a lock, you're not hauling your gear a short way; you are hauling it the length of football fields. How I was going to survive the afternoon and reach St. Louis by nightfall remained a mystery.

I sat in the dirt trying to decide whether I should give up, hang tight, and have my parents come get me, or to push on and embrace the challenge. There appeared to be what looked like a gazebo about a hundred yards from where I sat, so I shouldered my gear and staggered forth, hoping to find shade, and with any luck, a bathroom.

I was not fortunate enough to find anything more than shade, but my luck changed when no more than five minutes after reaching the gazebo, Scott, one of the lock operators, came to my aid in a golf cart. We packed the cart down, and I held my SUP out to the side. Miss Sunshine stretched longer than the cart by two feet front and back. "What are you doing out here?" "Trying not to die." I said.

"You look a little parched. Would you like to come indoors for some AC?"

"That would be awesome!" I said. "I've always wanted to see how these things work."

The last time I was inside a lock station was after Cora and I almost drowned. So seeing the inner workings was actually the last thing on my mind, fluids was what I was craving. When Scott opened the door, my knees buckled. It was like an igloo inside. He offered me some water and gave me the grand tour. It was quite a sight looking down on the river. I told them about my journey and spent a few more minutes in light conversation. When my body reached a reasonable temperature, I thanked the operators and then expressed my urgency to press on if I was going to make St. Louis by nightfall.

"Do you guys know of any convenience stores nearby where I can stock up on some more drinks?"

"The closest one is about ten miles away," said one of the operators, "but we can help you out."

He took me into the break room, opened the refrigerator, and I beheld such beauty it made my eyes misty. The shelves where packed full of ice-cold Mt. Dew, Dr. Pepper, Gatorade, and water. For five dollars, they let me take as much as I could carry (they offered it free, but I wanted to make a donation). I pulled each sweaty can out of its frosty den and touched it to my face, caressing the precious like Smeagle with his precious ring. I thanked them for their gracious hospitality and Scott helped me load my gear onto the golf cart and chauffeured me to the other side of the lock. After securing everything to the SUP, I waved at the guys who were watching from the station and then pushed hard for the Gateway Arch.

I paddled well into the night with an amber moon as my guide, hanging low and brilliant just above the surface of the

Miss. I sailed through the swift merging of the Illinois and Missouri rivers into the Mississippi, and reached St. Louis just before midnight.

It's funny how things change. It used to be that paddling at night made me nervous. Doesn't matter now. If you endure something long enough, it simply becomes who you are. Fear is gone. Routine sets in.

For seventy-five and some odd days, I'd been paddling the old black waters. The stories, the people... they danced about in my dreams while the Mississippi winds caressed my tent. In many ways, by the time I reached the Gateway Arch, the emotional and spiritual leg of my journey was complete. If the ultimate purpose of my river adventure hung solely on records and recognition, then I should continue. But it didn't. The purpose was to share, heal, and open myself to life once more. Mission accomplished.

As I approached the north end of St. Louis, my dad sent me a text that they had safely landed. Now, the daunting task of finding me in the dark. I used the GPS on my cell phone (something I've done only a handful of times over a thousand miles) but the battery was getting low. I reached a small, public boat ramp just north of St. Louis, but before I could call my dad and tell him where I was, the light went out. I panicked in the dark for a bit until a truck pulled up and a man got out to hitch up his boat that was bobbing in the water at the base of the ramp. He was kind enough to lend me a hand and helped to guide my parents into my waiting arms. They plucked me from the river and I spent the next three days resting and relaxing with my family. I would sleep in until noon and then they would feed me Mom and Dad listened as I painted story after story of dams, detours, Wildman, and Cora. I described this new leg of the river that I was battling. My dad spent three weeks with me in some of the most beautiful country in northern Minnesota. Now, I was in the Big Muddy.

On the morning of our third and final day together, my parents drove me to a launch site just north of the Gateway Arch. I hugged them both as tightly as possible without hurting them and then we took some pictures together. As I waded into the water, I gazed up at the 630' high sculpture, and smiled. A short year ago, weeks before I tried to die, I sat inside the Arch looking down upon the Mississippi River. I had no idea the horrors that were about ensue... the suffering and the potential loss of life. I watched as the muddy waters meandered southward without knowledge of the intimate bond we would soon share. Now, that very river was transporting me into a new chapter in my life. A Mighty chapter.

I entered the water and waved at my parents one last time. They watched as I paddled past the Gateway Arch and into the final leg of my quest.

ooo

River life quickly fell into its simple monotony.

After the news reports in Quincy, I became a minor celebrity through Hannibal, Louisiana, and into St. Louis.

People would wave from shore and come out in their boats to greet the miracle man paddling on their river.

Some would say, "You look like Jesus walking on water!"

"Jesus had hair," I replied.

They had a point, though. From a distance, it's hard to distinguish three inches of foam between your feet from the river, so I can see where the appearance of "walking on water" was accurate.

The distance between towns continued to be a factor that I refused to respect nor prepare for. I would run out of water by early afternoon and go thirsty for hours. I already carried the burden of chronic pain. Dehydrating my muscles only compounded the problem. My feet would swell so badly that I'd have to sit down and put them in the water. I'd stand up and paddle for another hour then repeat.

I moved into several days of tedium after my parents' departure. I stuck to a routine and made little effort to share my story; there was nobody there to share it with anyways. I became robotic in my mission to put miles behind me. The currents quickened their pace after the Missouri emptied into the Mississippi and I was doubling my miles in comparison to what I did north of St. Louis. I wasn't eating right or drinking enough fluids, and I would often become fatigued and disoriented. My campsites became increasingly barren and lonely, like I was an exile or in a Mad Max film.

What I needed was a lively encounter to break the monotony.

At the end of another long day, I pulled into the town of Genevieve reeling from thirst. I left my gear in the sand without a thought for its safety, and staggered down the road in search of water. Genevieve was eerily quiet. The amber remains of dusk cast a wicked glow, bouncing light between buildings. It was like a ghost town. Nothing was open and there were no convenience stores in sight. While wandering up and down the quiet streets, I noticed the same truck more than once and had a suspicious feeling that it was trailing me. He was in front of me. He passed me. He pulled out of the side street. He would stop and stare. He must have been circling. How else would he be everywhere at once? Finally, he stopped, rolled down his window and asked, "Hey? Aren't you the guy on the news?"

I told him I was and then expressed my desperate need for water, so he offered to take me to the gas station. He was a chubby, round-faced fellow, with a full beard. We'll call him

"Bill." On the way to the gas station, I asked Bill if he knew of a place that I could set up camp without someone kicking me out in the middle of the night.

"Well," he scratched underneath his chin with the backs of his fingers, "I just moved my niece out of my house today. You're welcome to the spare bedroom." The furniture in the back of his truck legitimized the story. For two months, I had received an outpouring of kindness from the people of the river, so I didn't hesitate to take him up on the offer. I told him where my gear was and he drove back to the river, so I could load up.

"How far from the river is your house?"

"Oh, just up the road."

We pulled away from the riverbank and I watched through the passenger side mirror as the Mississippi grew smaller and smaller before eventually disappearing from sight.

Just up the road apparently meant twenty miles away. We pulled off the highway onto a country road that morphed into a single lane road that eventually became a dirt road. Civilization disappeared, choked out by the forest. Bill continued to drive deeper into the woods until we entered a clearing that housed a circle of mobile homes. My rational mind disappeared and I began to quietly panic. I came through a horrific ordeal in the hospital, survived the dam, only to die at the hands of Missouri gypsies.

Bill pulled up to the first trailer in the group and turned off the truck. Without prompting, he picked up some of my bags, carried them into the trailer, and immediately led me to the bathroom.

"I have to go talk to a friend, but I thought you might want to take a shower."

I'm a victim of my own insane imagination and it was

currently set on overdrive. I put my bag in the spare bedroom, paying close attention to where I hid my gun. I went to the bathroom and took a shower in a tub with no curtain. When I got out, I heard someone in the other room. I emerged from the bathroom to find my host sitting in his recliner watching TV in nothing but boxer shorts with a little dog in his lap.

He was watching *America's Got Talent* and invited me to sit down. At this point, all I wanted to do was lock myself in the room and sleep, wake up, and get back on the river, but I didn't want to be rude so I joined him for a bit. We made small talk during commercials. This is when that I noticed the magazine rack behind his chair.

Tucked within was an issue of *BEAR* and on the cover stood a big, burly lumberjack-looking fellow without a shirt. Suddenly, I felt very claustrophobic. I was trapped in a trailer in the middle of the woods. Even if I wanted to split, my board and gear would be too much to carry for twenty miles; that's implying that I could find my way back.

Discreetly, I took a picture of the magazine with my phone and sent a text to Cora with the caption, "HELP." I was trying to make light of my situation and knew she would have a good laugh. She replied, "Oh, he's harmless (smiley face)"

Bill kept up with the lively chitchat for about an hour. When I found an opening, I thanked him for the hospitality and explained that the day's paddle was exhausting and that I'd like to go to bed.

His demeanor changed instantaneously. I felt it in the air. It was thick and uncomfortable.

He stood up, bare belly and boxers, and motioned for me to follow him to the guest room. As he opened the door, I choked back a groan. It was a hoarder's haven and somewhere in the middle of that funky clutter was a bed. All I wanted was to be back under a bridge or in my tent or lying on my board, in the dark, floating down the river. All the above would be sanctuary from this place.

"Well, I really appreciate this." I managed to speak. "Good night, then."

Bill stood in the room, not saying a word; he just stared at me for about a billion seconds.

I was not scared of Buffalo Bill and his little dog. I knew I could handle myself with him if things got ugly. What made me nervous were the ten mobile homes that surrounded his, filled with "who knows who." Maybe Bill owned them all and filled them with mannequins and dolls, and they all had names and he went and visited them and had tea and brought me to his house to take my skin... or something?

"Is this going to be OK for you?"

Thank God, he spoke. He was freaking me out staring at me like that.

"Yeah, it's great. I'm going to crash now, thanks again." More staring.

Now, I was getting irritated so I stared back. I figured locking eyes might drag out his intentions. He looked at the floor, back at me, up at the ceiling, back at me and then his lips moved.

"So, you know I'm gay right?" *Dammit.*

"Um, well, I don't judge. We are who we are and I believe people deserve to live their life free of judgment and ignorance. But, I'm not gay." I babble when I'm nervous.

He kept his eyes on me.

I waited for another billion seconds. What could come after such a question? Maybe he couldn't care less if I was gay or not. Why was I thinking of Cora all of a sudden? Was it because I knew she would be laughing right now? I knew she would be! Harmless, she told me. The guy was harmless!

My ignorance to his intentions would soon be over.

"So... how about a BJ?"

The words hung in space between us like a cartoon bubble. I felt beads of sweat forming on my brow. I must have turned several shades of red because he started to back pedal towards the door.

"No, thank you."

"Ok then, if you change your mind..."

"I won't."

Bill left the room and I closed the door, reinforced it with my gear, loaded my gun, and sat on the bed surrounded by clutter. I hoped that my rejection wouldn't fuel some kind of rage, forcing him to fetch the rest of the gypsies. I kept a keen ear out for banjo music. I eased myself into the rickety bed and called Cora. I had to wait five minutes for her to stop laughing before I could get a word in. "You said he was harmless!" Another round of laughter.

"I said he was harmless. I never said he wasn't horny!"

I managed to sleep for a couple of hours and the next morning, Bill returned me to the river. It *was* a completely harmless situation. A hilarious situation, but harmless. My internal overreaction to my dilemma was a side effect of a spastic imagination. At least I was able to entertain Cora and I had another story to tell The Monsters on Real Radio 104.1 during my Friday update.

Bill was the last person I stayed with on the river. After my ordeal in the woods, I returned to several days of camping alone on the muddy banks of the Mighty.

RIVER JOURNAL,
SEPTEMBER 12, 2011

it seems as if i am never satisfied
with the present. in the north, i
complained about mosquitos, deer
flies and the tedious twists and
turns of the Mighty. now, those
beautiful landscapes are all i can
think about down here in the big
muddy. it's lonely below st. louis
and sometimes i wonder if i will
be on this river forever. live in
the present, Matt. When you are
home, you will crave the solitude
of these southern waters...

19

Cape G

Cora was coming back for me.

At the end of our two weeks together, I thought for sure I'd become nothing more than a memory, especially after a drunken email, but the phone calls continued when she returned to Florida. Obviously, Cora did not scare easily. I felt sure she would leave me to the Mighty, and to memory, but it appeared that I had the same effect on her as she did me. She met with my parents back home in Orlando and expressed a desire to follow me the rest of the way by car to help carry the supplies I would need to survive the ever-increasing distances between river towns. It was music to my mom's ears—and mine. I could not wait to see her again, to hold her... to continue falling. There was a break in her work schedule, giving her the green light to spend my final few weeks next to me. She would be my sexy support vehicle. She would be there at the end. She would be the one to bring me home.

There was no shortage of praise and support from the people of the river. They would tell me things like, "It's not fair; those other two boys ahead of you had sponsorship and support." Well, so have I. For three months, I received the waters of life from more people than I can remember, and now, one more angel was coming to my rescue. No way I could ever take credit for paddling the Mighty alone. I'd often wonder how my competitors fared on the lower Mississippi. She was a harsh mistress south of St. Louis. Even with my new SUP, I could barely pack the necessities needed for survival. I still had to watch the weight. I missed the convenience of being able to pull over whenever necessary. I could always find some sort of town north of the Arch. At times, I would be tempted to contact Dave or Alex and inquire about what was ahead of me. What did they face? Where did they stop? What potential hazards were waiting for me? I never did. I was never the type who wanted to know what lie over the horizon until I could see it for myself. One thing I knew for sure-The Mighty was going to fight me all the way.

It seemed as if the river barges had grown dramatically as well. I thought they were big north of the Arch. In the south, they were gargantuan. To put it into perspective, a river barge is a flat-bottomed boat used to transport goods through canals and rivers. Each barge can hold fifteen times that of a rail car and sixty times greater than a tractor-trailer and that's just one. They are linked together, sometimes as much as five wide and seven long. Thirtyfive barges full of cargo—simply amazing. Supposedly, they are small in comparison to what I would experience farther south, as ocean-going vessels entered the river. I'd be a dwarf among giants.

At night, I'd tell Cora of the river—the barges, the isolation, the physical exertion—and it solidified her desire to come to me. She gave me a date of departure and after consulting the map, I made plans to meet her in Cape Girardeau, MO.

For the next week, I endured a strenuous routine of sleep,

paddle, sleep, paddle. I was up early and paddled 8-10 hours a day. The currents kept a steady pace. When I paddled close to shore, I could see how quickly I was moving as the earth rolled by, but I stuck to the channel where it was the fastest. Taking the channel meant dealing with barge traffic. A head-on collision that I would never win.

The night before Cora's arrival, I settled in Red Star Park, under a gazebo, and set up camp. I sat in my tent and felt the hard ground beneath me. I pictured her spending fifteen plus hours driving to me just to sleep on that hard ground, or in the back of her SUV. It simply would not do. I wanted our reunion to be special, so I ventured further into Cape G in search of better options. I wanted to whisk her away into a night of fine dining and 5-star accommodations, but I was a water bum with limited funds, so I made do with what I had to offer.

I remembered her telling me how much she loved hash brown casserole from Cracker Barrel during one of our random conversations. She spoke of it with such passion; it was hilarious. I searched my phone and to my surprise, there was a Cracker Barrel a few miles away. They really are *everywhere*. According to Google Maps, there was a humble, but comfortable motel across the street from the restaurant so I booked a room. My plan would be, while she was settling in, to go pick up dinner, complete with hash brown casserole, and have a romantic dinner waiting for her in the room. I realized it was a bit on the pathetic side, but it was all I had to offer.

Satisfied with the plan, I returned to camp and crawled into my tent. Cora called me from the road singing, *I Drove all Night* into the receiver, hopped up on pumpkin spice lattes. We talked and laughed as she closed the gap between us until I eventually fell asleep.

The next day, I paced impatiently outside my tent while guiding her in on the phone. I searched the horizon for her silver

Mazda and when it came into sight, I waved my arms until she came to a stop beside me. She sprang from the car, into my arms, and wrapped her legs around my waist. I was never letting go. I laughed when I saw her car. It was an SUV all right, but a bit on the small side. It was about the same length as my SUP. Fortunately, I carried ratchet straps with me. We rolled up some towels to act as a barrier between my board and her roof, and I cranked the straps down to a comfortable degree of security. Confident that the SUP wouldn't catch an updraft and transport us to OZ, I told her to get in. She was prepared to camp in the car each night, but today I had a surprise. She was dropping her life for me, putting everything on hold to see me through the worst of the river and I was not going to let her sleep in the car that first night. She was going to have a hot shower, her favorite food, and a soft bed.

We got to the room and while she showered off her road trip, I ran across the street to pick up her feast. She stepped out of the bathroom and a big smile stretched across her face when she saw me pull a tub of hash brown casserole from a big brown Cracker Barrel bag.

For the rest of the night, we relaxed in each other's arms and I mentally prepared myself for the final push. My body was exhausted, and truth be told, I was ready to go home.

I had beautiful stories, another near-death at the dam, and my tale of resurrection reached many. It was a life changing three months and I could have returned home with Cora with a full heart and a smile. But that wasn't going to happen. I had to finish. It was something I had to do for me. Though the next several weeks on the river would be scorching, long, and uneventful, it would be where I would truly come face to face with the man I had become after my brush with death.

We left Cape G behind us and sailed on to Memphis.

Cora would drop me off in the morning and frantically try to locate me at the end of the day, navigating dangerous back roads in search of landmarks where we could rally. After the day's paddle was over, we would retire to whatever campground or state park she tracked down while I was paddling. I would prep our bed in the back of her SUV and hang sheer bug nets over the windows while she made me supper on an electric hot plate. Often we would fall asleep laughing and watching movies on her laptop. I suffered greatly in the hospital and the months that followed. It was so nice to be happy again. If one of my reasons for being on the Mississippi was to find my smile again... I considered it accomplished.

I kicked my days on the river into overdrive. In two weeks, I paddled through Cairo, Hickman, New Madrid, and Caruthersville, leaving behind the states of Missouri, Illinois, and Kentucky to enter Arkansas and Tennessee. John, a friend from Orlando, was in Memphis for an orientation. He was a pilot and worked many years for a commercial operation. We stopped for a few days to congratulate him and have some fun. Then it was back to routine.

The Mighty was breaking me down more and more each day. If I had to secure campsites, food and water, it would have been too much. I was so thankful for Cora. I could barely move at the end of the day and had a rough time waking up. I dumped the bulk of my medication a month back, and every day I feared the return of disease. I was thankful for the river north of St. Louis. It was good to experience a place where folks used the Mississippi for recreation. She's forgotten in the South, except for her commercial value. Muddy, dark and deep. I navigated my remaining days in southern humidity and solitude, then, would rest in the arms of Cora by night.

During those lonely days, I would often reflect on the

first ten hours of my journey. The brutal twenty miles that threatened to end me after day one. I thought about what I would have missed had I given up—the stories, the memories—they flickered, one after another, on a mental slide projector. The mellow yellow, cone-shaped light illuminated the back of my skull as the memories clicked into place. I paused at some before moving on to the next.

I wouldn't have had those precious weeks with my father, taking pictures under Paul Bunyan and Babe. He wouldn't have been there, waving at every intersecting bridge or to share meals and stories by night. There would be no Detour, no Jordan Davis. No moonshine and rope swings. No happy-go-lucky tubers from Elk River. The Apperts, no Chris from the Yacht Club. No Wildman on a Harley. The heroes of Lock and Dam 16. Jeff and his boat and birthday celebrations in the Quad Cities. Their faces will forever wave in my memory like cornstalks in the crimson Iowan dusk; a sea of souls that now shares my heart.

Most of all, if I would have quit... there would be no Cora.

The world between quitting and moving forward can make a profound impact on our lives. Some will say, "Yes, but you would never know." But I do know. I will always know the product of my decision to get up and face the river again.

It's amazing. Twenty miles had turned into 1,500; I still rambled on.

The lower Miss was a treacherous part of the river, and devastatingly lonely. My feet hurt from gripping my board with ape-like toes. There would be low-lying rock jetties that would poke out into the channel. I assumed they were there to divert the river. Whatever the reasons, I wouldn't see them until I was practically on top of them. I'd lose balance and was pummeled by the rocks as the current dragged me along. I held tight to a faltering heart while paddling through Mississippi, Arkansas, and

Louisiana. I wonder if such things are typical for all adventures-a
faltering heart near the end. Perhaps it's a part of the pilgrim's
progress. Could it be true that if a journey is at its worst near
the end it makes accomplishment that much sweeter? Makes a
certain kind of sense.

I would often fall into singular thinking, concerned only for
my own necessities and daily goals, forgetting that there was an
angel following me by land. For me, my direction was simple...
head south. Cora, however, had to navigate for hours, searching
endless dead end roads for a glimpse of the river. A glimpse of
me. She had no idea how to connect with me and no way of
knowing if I was "alright and upright".

Cell signal was sporadic in those desolate southern parts,
so coordinating for a pickup was part skill, mostly luck. I could
pull to shore anywhere but would be miles from any road. Every
evening was a frantic struggle to connect before the sunlight
abandoned us. When we found each other, it was like meeting
her for the first time all over again.

At night, after camp was set and our bellies were full, we'd
snuggle under the stars and Cora would share her daily journal
entries with me. It gave me a unique perspective of river life
from the road.

This particular entry was one of my favorites:

Cora's Journal, September 14, 2011
The Forgotten

*Today is one of the rare moments when i actually have
internet service in Vicksburg. i really do appreciate
this river town in Mississippi. a place that has finally
filled my expectations of what a river town should
be, littered with cute shops and restaurants. a place*

where people drive from all over the us to appreciate the history of the river. in addition, it completely redeemed my feelings about the state of Mississippi. Prior to Vicksburg, unlike the towns north of st. louis, deep southern towns seem unloved. it's a sad realization that america still has its poor parts; it leaves one feeling depressed as you drive by. even the weather seems sad. it's been crying rain for the last several days. The roads are muddy and the campsites are closed and flooded. as we travel from town to town, each place seems more rundown and deserted than the last. They seem haunted. Houses are falling down, stores are empty, and gas stations are dry and unattended. it's a little nerve-wracking when you are on an empty tank and the last three stations on your GPs are out of business in the middle of cornfields. The ones that are still open look like a biology lab. next to bags of pigskin rinds, there are big glass jars filled with pink fluid of pig's feet, quail eggs, and some other animal anatomy that i couldn't identify. i've noticed that no one plays on the river as much in the deep south. it seems neglected, ignored, and abandoned. There are no children playing in the water, no fisherman fishing in their boats, no boaters enjoying a weekend cruise. nope, just barges. big, ugly, rusty-looking metal barges filled with corn, beans, and rice.

Because everything is so desolate, after i drop Matthew off, i'm usually filled with anxiety. My days are spent driving around on dirt roads, private property, and looking for "Where's Waldo" to pop through on his board somewhere along the way. The river is set deep within the land, nestled in a mess of brush and trees. Finding an opening usually led me to a levy that looked down from a hill into a mess of shrubbery with only the sound, not sight, of the Mississippi River.

There are few and far-between dock options (to drop him off and pick him up), with tons of farmland between the roads and the great river. These parts also leave me feeling quite lonely. i feel like i'm in a third-world country because internet and cell phone service are scarce. i miss talking to my friends or kayaking in the water beside my crazy paddle boarder, enjoying our daily conversations and listening to music while floating down the river. i am thankful that i traded my kayak for my car and i brought my two doggies who provide me with my only companionship during the day. i spend my days worrying about the river challenges Matthew is facing while i drive on dusty dirt roads just hoping to find an opening to check up on him. i usually spend a half tank of gas on miles of disappointment. no luck. instead, i seem to navigate straight into curious old men that follow me in the backcountry in their trucks, dogs chasing my car, and signs that warn that i will be shot at if i trespass on their property. The good ol' south! Once in a great while, i'm able to find a barge docking point at a grain tower. When i do, the dogs and i wait for hours. My mind starts to fill up with crazy thoughts during this time. it makes me nervous that Matthew has to share the river with these enormous barges who occupy and own the black water of the Mississippi. He looks like a tiny speck floating next to them.

With each passing day, i have collected more disturbing memories of unsettling visuals of Matthew taking off on his board every morning. as each rainy day passes, i sit in my car watching him on his paddleboard until he disappears, and then my quest to find camp and checkpoints begins. at each send off, i normally take a picture with my cellphone and text them to his parents, but lately, i have decided to not share my scary visual with them.

The weather hasn't been kind. The rain is competing with the wind. The wind is competing with the waves. at one of the turn offs, i got a visual of Matt. He was laying on his board, belly down, clutching on for dear life while swirling past a whirlpool. There is nothing i can do but sit silently in my car, far from shore, watching him struggle and praying for his safe return to land. even with these obvious obstacles, and the physical pain that he faces, he refuses to give up. it is raining. i see dark gray clouds with sounds of distant thunder and lightning. i beg him not to get in. i fear i won't find an opening to find him and he will drift in oblivion. but, nevertheless, his thirst for finishing is unquenchable and i lose the battle of convincing him to stay on shore.

The farther down we travel, acts of kindness seem to be less predominate than they were in the north, but i attribute that to the desolate landscape. For the last couple of weeks, the river has been relentless on him. Rain, whirlpools, winds, and water currents fight him with every paddle stroke. The river current is faster after st. louis. The river now carries him 50 to 70 miles per day, instead of 20-30. He has to wear a life-jacket because there have been several times his board has tipped over due to combatting the weather, along with rocky jetties, currents, and barges.

Matthew's emotional motivations seem to be off lately. He now feels that completing the Mississippi is more for personal satisfaction instead of a need to share his story. The shorelines were empty and the river only represented obstacles. i knew this wasn't the case. His story still needed to be told with reminders that miracles still exist; especially in the southern parts where everything seems to be forgotten. a reminder arrived in the next town called Lake Providence, Louisiana. it came in the form of a cute little coffee shop oasis called, "Jehovah Java." it was owned by a pastor named, brother don. He was a proud, white bearded grandpa who typed up little bible verses on paper and passed them out with your order. The day we arrived, he also informed all of his customers of the birth of his new granddaughter, who was born earlier that day. i still remember his apple cheeks and eyes filled with twinkles as he talked about his new-found joy. as we were eating, i started inquiring about campsites and places to see and brother don began asking about the surfboard on top of my car. This led to Matt telling him about his mighty journey. brother don enjoyed hearing Matt's crazy story so much, he called a friend who owned a local hotel and he offered us a free night. Then, brother don told us to stop by the coffee shop in the morning and he would give us free coffee before returning to the river! That little coffee shop really lived up to its name!

Brother don, thank you for helping Matthew and thank you for sending us on our way with a delicious order of Peppermint Patty and Milky Way coffee. We smiled as we drank our little sips of heaven down to the river.

Half way happiness at the St. Louis Arch!

Always a party on the Mississippi.

A southern boy back home in the south.

Making peace with an old friend.

RIVER JOURNAL,
SEPTEMBER 18, 2011

John V! so good to hang with you in Memphis, buddy! Good luck in flight school. i'll never forget what you always say to me when i'm about to take off on some crazy adventure. "There will always be people in your life who tell you that you can't do something, and others who cheer you on." i'm paraphrasing, but we're usually a couple beers in when talking about such things. Looking forward to some wings and brew when we both return to the sunshine state in the fall!

20

A Fragile State

The rain begins to fall—a slow drizzle at first—and I know by the sound I am close to home. Southern rain has a feel to it. Storms approach in the bright blue with a mighty fury and then disappear without so much as a goodbye, leaving the asphalt to steam and hiss. That's how I remember them back home. However, this storm may set in a while.

Suddenly, I grow exhausted and sad. It is a happy sad, a kind of melancholy. As I approach the end of my journey down the Mississippi river, it is hard to fathom how far I've come. I have reached levels of exhaustion that I never knew were possible. Waves of mental and physical exhaustion. I am bone weary. Weary has a certain feel doesn't it? A tired feeling that is soul deep. I was barely half a man when I pushed off from the headwaters four months ago. I was still very sick with disease and lacking the muscle strength I had been accustomed to before Costa Rica. But the paddle has helped me to fill out a bit I'm happy to say, (maybe a little too much around the waist thanks to the generosity of the river folk), still, I was never prepared for the magnanimity of this adventure.

It has been a lonely, monotonous stretch from Memphis to

Vicksburg, Vicksburg to Natchez, and Natchez on into Baton
Rouge, where I now rest before the final miles between here and
the end of my river. Baton Rouge means "red stick" in French.
Which is basically what I am, thanks to the southern sun. A
wind-battered, red stick struggling to reach its journey's end.

River hospitality remained a constant from northern
Minnesota on down to Louisiana where I've been graced with
yet another free spot to set up camp. Cora hasn't been feeling
well since Memphis, so it's important to me to provide her with
comfortable accommodations; even if our shelter was the back
of a Mazda SUV, I could at least see to it that where we parked
was safe so she could rest comfortably in my arms. The cool river
breeze would coax us to sleep. And I do declare, it was some of
the finest sleep this side of the Mississippi.

Often, she'd fall asleep first, and I would lie awake in quiet
darkness, listening to her breath while reflecting on the miles
traveled. Baton Rouge would be the last major city I'd visit before
reaching New Orleans. I've passed through the quiet north,
home to nothing more than river otters, beavers, and kayaks.
Soon after, I shared space with sporadic recreational crafts until
the river teamed with them. Following the first lock, I found
myself paddling alongside massive river barges, gaining inches
and hours through relentless headwinds, and now, in the South, I
find myself dwarfed by a new beast in the form of mighty ocean-
going vessels.

Over two thousand miles on a paddleboard. Huckleberry
Finn, eat your happy, adventure-loving heart out.

As I approached the Jazz-pumping, spicy gumbo of one of
my favorite cities in America, a sense of completeness began to
knock at my chest, eager to take refuge in my heart, and begged
the question... what now?

Most believe the end of the Mississippi River is in New

Orleans, but there is a small (small in comparison to the distance the three of us paddleboarders had already traveled, but still over a hundred miles) portion that winds through the marsh before her life is extinguished in the Gulf of Mexico. That is where my predecessors had made their stand. It was the place where a distance record was made, and then quickly broken by another.

Alex Linnel from Minnesota already claimed the title of "First Person to Paddleboard the Length of the Mississippi" and set the world's long distance record for paddle boarding. England's Dave Cornthwaite claimed that title a few weeks later by paddling a bit farther from the mouth of The Muddy into the green gulf below. However, Dave did it alone with nothing but his board and sixty lbs. of gear strapped to the front. The title of "Longest Distance Record on a Stand-Up Paddleboard" belongs to him, and I hope it stays that way for a very long time.

Grant me pardon if this sounds like I am knocking Alex's accomplishment because it is nowhere near my intentions. Alex took a significant journey. He said he was going to paddle the Mississippi River and he did. He was the first in history to do so. Twenty-one years old and the rightful owner of a job well done. I give my deepest respect to both of these men, for they are remarkable individuals.

But you see, records are made to be broken; it was the latter title I desired so much. I wanted to be Chris Columbus discovering new worlds. I wanted to know what it felt like to be "that guy"—the one who did it first. It almost robbed the simple joy of taking a new journey. And that would have been such a tragedy because it's the journey itself, and the joy of such experience, that we take home with us at the end.

Once it became painfully obvious that Alex was leaving this old man safely behind, I began to move into the realm of acceptance that my original desire would never come to fruition.

After Dave lapped me, I sulked in third place for a spell until I realized, even though I was in third place, I could still have the distance record by simply paddling a foot past Dave's final destination. I would have my title. I would have my name in the book, and I would have been a shallow man who had learned nothing about the adventure he was destined to take.

I remembered two months back when Cora and I had our first lengthy conversation on the phone and she spoke of her feelings towards my journey. She told me that whenever she closed her eyes and thought of me on the river, there were three lights floating down the river, and out of the three lights, the one in last place was the brightest. This helped me to understand what my journey was all about, and it had nothing to do with titles or records. I was fulfilling my mission by being a light upon dark waters. By sharing my story of hope with the people of the river and bearing witness that there are still things in this world that remain unexplainable, I was bringing healing into hearts that needed a miracle and they were giving the same back to me: healing my soul with each mile paddled.

Cora wasn't saying that I was better than those men—nothing could be further from the truth. She was mealy expressing that my trip was of a different motivation. Alex was striving to be the first in a major accomplishment. Dave is a career adventurer who desired to live a life beyond the ordinary. Both men were taking their voyages, unselfishly, with others in mind and had set up charities they were supporting with every mile.

My journey was about being born again.

As I drew closer to New Orleans, I knew I would not be going any farther. Those final miles belong to my friend Dave. He earned them and I was not going to selfishly paddle an inch past him. I found what I was looking for, and my personal course was near completion.

I've paddled for more miles than I or anyone else in my life ever expected. What more could I ask from a man who just twelve months ago had less than forty-eight hours to live?

RIVER JOURNAL,
SEPTEMBER 23, 2011 FINAL
ENTRY

A journey begins and a journey
ends. There were days on the river
that felt like an eternity. I wish I
had enjoyed them more, but there
are no regrets. it will soon to be
over... and I will be going home. i
will hold the people of the river in a
special place, down deep, forever. as
you navigate through this wildly
beautiful and treacherous thing we
call life, don't forget to slow down
once in awhile and actually live it.

"The key to immortality is to first
live a life worth remembering."
—Bruce Lee

21

Where the River Meets the Sea

I **was around** ten years old when my dad decided he wanted to run a 5k race and invited me to join him. I wanted to be with my dad all day every day, so I was thrilled. For weeks, we trained, running the bike trails through our neighborhood, sometimes by day, sometimes by night, and sometimes in the rain. Nighttime was my favorite. I hated going to bed and being outside, running wild with my dad, was a rare treat. After our jog, we would jump in the pool and it was just fun times for me all around.

When race day arrived, I had my usual cocky confidence (evidently it started young) that we would not only finish the race, but would be elbow to elbow at the front of the line. The gun fired and the race began. I ran with conviction! I ran with gusto! And by the time the first mile sauntered by, I could barely run at all... and we were the only two left at the end of the line. By the second mile, there was a war waging in my tiny shoes begging me to give up. My dad could have gone ahead with ease, but, as usual, his desire was to be next to his son. By mile three, I was done, but my dad encouraged me to put the race aside

and simply concentrate on running and at least finish without
walking a single step.

"Keep running, son. Don't stop until you cross the finish
line."

It was probably more like a clumsy power walk, but I kept
up the jog. The other runners had long since finished their race
and were enjoying hot chocolate in the cool night air, while
I struggled through mile number five and the end of mine. I
stumbled across the finish line and into my dad's proud arms,
but I pushed him aside and began to sulk. "I'm last. I can't believe
I came in last. I'm such a failure."

My dad has said many things to me throughout my years of
fumbling and flopping from childhood to present days. Some
things I remember; some things I don't, but I'll never forget what
he said while sipping hot chocolate under the stars with puffs
of warm vapor billowing into the cold air after every word. He
placed his hand on my shoulder, using the other to turn my chin,
forcing me to look into his eyes and said...

"Son, you are never a failure as long as you finish the race."

ooo

I got out of the car and planted a kiss on Cora's soft, ruby lips.

"See you in the Big Easy," I winked.

She waved and snapped photos as I made my way towards the
Mighty for the last time. I descended the rocky incline towards
the river's edge and placed my SUP in the water. I waved and
flashed a smile Cora's way then popped to my feet and felt that
familiar flow.

"I'll miss that feeling," I thought to myself. Some days I
wanted nothing to do with that muddy river. Now, I could feel
the precious moments of lazy days dripping off my paddle, and
soon they would drip no more. I knew in my heart that when I

returned to land life, I would crave those monotonous days on the Mighty.

I was a crockpot of emotion the moment I hit the water. I felt exhausted and stretched to my limits. I was frightened at the thought of "what next," but happy to discover "what next." Mostly, it was the realization that my four-month hourglass was dropping its final grains of sand.

Four months funneled into a few more hours.

I struggled with the letdown that I was not going to be the first, and then I struggled with the importance of setting a record even if I were not number one. I struggled with the decision to end my journey in New Orleans. It's safe to say I struggled all the way down the Mississippi. The Mighty fought me the whole way. Out of a hundred and twenty plus days, I could count on both hands the ones where the wind was at my back and the fates aligned to create a perfect pace. The rest, a fight for every mile, battling headwinds, rough waters, disease, and constant pain... and I loved it.

By the time I reached New Orleans, scratch that, by the time I reached St. Louis, I had a woman who loved me and more stories than I ever imagined possible. I wanted to quit after the first day. To come this far was a dead man's dream.

Cora once told me that she didn't believe I was on this river because of a broken heart but for a broken spirit. "A broken heart is much easier to fix," she said.

I would have to agree because my spirit had all but disappeared before this journey began. She also told me that as I made my way down the Mighty Miss, I would drop the darkness into the black waters and slowly pick up the pieces of my soul. I believe I have.

You may not realize this... but I am you.

I'm your anger, I'm your fear, I'm your elation, I'm your bliss.

I am your manic, I am your depression. I'm your parts that are abused and used. I am your hot mess. I am your train wreck. I am your marvel to behold and all things beautiful. I am your work of art. I am your forked-tongued liar and your seeker of all things true. I am your quitter and your victor.

I am human, as are you. We are connected. We are not alone.

If you met me on the river, if you shared in my life, or if you simply need some encouraging words from a man who knows darkness, please allow me to pass some earned wisdom as you float down your own mighty river. Stay strong in the face of hopelessness; even to the point where you feel there is nothing left to give and you just want to let go. Please, do not. All it takes is a day. The difference of one day can be the beginning of a new life.

Through my near-death, I began a new chapter. I wanted to conquer a river, but instead I found harmony with nature. I wanted to wither away in darkness and self-pity, but I found the light. I wanted to drown all that was good and merciful about me so I wouldn't have to feel anymore—instead, I found someone who showed me mercy and brought all feeling back to my heart. I shared in the lives of many, these people of the river, and in the end I discovered my true purpose for attempting such an insane endeavor was to tell my story.

Pain, struggle, heartache... they are as much a part of life as smiles and laughs. The two must embrace, for how would you truly relish the bright light of day without passing through the shadows of night. In a world where we expect concrete evidence before belief takes hold-where proof is in the touch, and sight is mandatory before the unseen appears—I am a walking testimony that not all things can be explained, miracles still exist, and love remains the most powerful force in the universe.

Travel has been a significant part of my transformation. So

much of what we come to fear in our lives is a product of televised accounts of random vile acts, but I tell you with earnest, I believe the good outweighs the evil. Travel has that effect. When one spends an entire lifetime in a place that is comfortable, in the company of like-minded individuals, it becomes increasingly difficult to discern what reality is from media propaganda. Home and familiar faces are a much-desired necessity in my life... like water... but the road has become my bread.

Am I an expert? Hardly. I'm not even a college graduate. But I've logged in over 40,000 miles on two wheels. I've also traveled using my thumb, hopping trains, and on a giant surfboard and the only dangers I ever faced that threatened to take my life were of my doing. Death will eventually come for us all; this knowledge should not bind us in fear to venture out into places unknown or hinder us from putting a little faith in humanity. There is good in this world, so much so, I often find myself overflowing because of another's kindness. Bad things happen, and you can spend your life weighing risk and avoiding the dark corners of the world. But in the end, it may be nothing more than a steamy pile of white bat poop in some obscure cave off a Central American coastline that will end your days on planet blue.

My final day on the Mississippi drew to an end with the New Orleans skyline an arm's length away. However, before I could reach the French Quarter, I found myself in a game of chicken with a mighty ocean liner. Refusing to quit, I pressed on through a deadly obstacle course of smoky metal ships until an Army Corps engineer trolled out in a small dingy and "forcefully" suggested that I get off the river. Cora, snapped a photo of me outside the Army Corps Station, and I ended my journey on the Mississippi.

I had visions of a grand party in New Orleans, and many of

my friends threatened to be there with me at the end, but people have enough to juggle in their own lives. I was more than thrilled with the reality that when the day was over, I would rest in Cora's arms and hers alone. With Cora I would end my journey, and, with her, I would begin a new one.

Before returning to Florida, we booked a room at a B&B near the French Quarter, and for the next three days, we played together in New Orleans, celebrating my accomplishment and daydreaming about our lives beyond the river. We slurped Hurricanes, stuffed ourselves with beignets, and spent nights strolling hand-in-hand through floating jazz notes popping from brass instruments like bubbles spilling over into damp streets.

She came out of nowhere and had become my everything.

In the end, there were no parties, no newspapers—just a quiet ride home with the Gulf to my right and a beauty behind the wheel to my left. All was good in the world.

Before I launched from the headwaters, a young woman spoke to me of making wishes and that my wish would come true by the time the waters that wet my ankles reached the sea. I made a wish that day that my life would change beyond my wildest dreams by the time I reached the Gulf.

Three months after my homecoming, Cora and I drove down to Key West where I married her beside green waters under a bright blue sky. She was my treasure at the end of an amazing adventure. She gave me purpose and a new chance at happiness, but even more than that—despite the doctors' testimony that due to the trauma I experienced in the hospital I would most likely never become a father—I became a daddy. We named him Aden, which means "little fire", for it is out of fire that we are forged to become like steel. Fourteen months later, a precious little girl… we named her Ella.

As far as Mississippi wishes are concerned... I think it's safe to say, my life has changed beyond my wildest dreams.

From the headwaters of the Mighty to the Big Easy, I searched around every corner for hope.... hope that a new life would be waiting. Hope that I would be forgiven and hope that I could make a difference. I never imagined it would turn out so beautiful.

Someday, when my children are older and facing the darkness that this world is sure to consume them with at times, I will tell them of a story that began at the edge of death to creating new life and somewhere in between... there was a river.

When their hearts are weary and heavy-laden and they so desperately wants to lie down and give up the fight, I will put my arms around them and tell them what their Papop told me many years ago at the headwaters of that mighty journey.

Simply put...

Never give up.

Epilogue

Fast-forward two years after my river journey, and you'll find me lounging in the parking lot of the Florida Hospital Cancer Center. My baby boy is cooing in his car seat as I sit with my windows down enjoying the first of autumn's cool breezes while scrolling through text messages. Cora and I recently discovered our second child, a baby girl, is on her way and I was relieved that my memoir was complete because things were about to get real!

It was—and always has been—my intention and motivation from the moment I was released from the hospital, through crippling, posttraumatic depression, to paddling the muddy Mississippi, to use proceeds from the book to pay forward what I could never repay. It was the beating heart behind every mile paddled. This is not because I am noble. Perhaps I'm trying to buy my way out of hell. Whatever. The problem is, I am in no way a philanthropist and I had zero idea where to begin. My disease is unusual and the way I almost died is unheard of. There is no Histoplasmosis foundation because they know how to help the common infected.

As my digital conversations continued, I noticed a car backing up in the parking spot in front of me. I could see through the glare in my windshield the soft glow of a bald head lying against the passenger side head rest. Bald heads are not uncommon. I see one in the mirror every day. I see them every other Tuesday when I bring Aden by the Cancer Center to visit his Nana at work, which was the very reason we were there on that particular day.

"How sad." I thought to myself as I continued thumbing away at my keypad. I wondered who the passenger was. A friend or a parent? Grandma or Grandpa?

The driver, a woman in her forties, (or perhaps looked so as a result of her plight), emerged from the car and rounded the front to the passenger side. She looked tired. The way the passenger's head was draped over the back of the seat, I could only assume exhaustion was normalcy between the two. I looked up from my phone, curious as to the identity of this unidentified patient, just as the driver extended both arms into the car and escorted a little girl from her seat. She was maybe six or seven. Mom helped stabilize the weary child with an arm around her hip. Before they began their walk to the doctor, the little girl looked up at her mom and her mom looked down. They smiled at each other as the mother planted a kiss on the child's forehead.

I gripped my steering wheel with both hands and struggled to hold back the tears. Then my son cooed once more from the back seat and I lost it. I watched as they disappeared into a sea of cars and I knew I would sell my soul to the devil himself if my child were to face such a challenge. To this day, it hurts my heart whenever I visualize that precious bald-headed little girl struggling to walk in her mother's arms. God damn cancer. That isn't an attempt at blasphemy. It is a prayer. God, please damn this wretched disease. I knew, in that moment, where I wanted proceeds from *Mighty* to go.

In memory of Jordan Davis, for my mother's lifelong service as a cancer nurse and as a survivor, and for every precious bald-headed child fighting on the front lines, I am donating a portion of every book sold to childhood cancer research.

It's not much—a pebble in a pond—but it's something, and with your help, I'll begin my quest to pay forward the extravagant generosity that was given to me in my hour of darkness.

Peace and Love!

Matt "The Tumbleweed" Crofton

Acknowledgments

My dear Mom and Dad. Without you, I would not have made it past my first day on the Mississippi. You remain my biggest fans. I'll love your forever, I'll like you for always. I hope I've kept things interesting.

A mighty thanks to everyone involved with sponsorship and delivery of my YOLO paddleboard: Jeff & Mitzi Archer, Tom Losee, Calvin and Debbie Blount, John Appel, Steve Gensolin, Jenna Hirt, and James Watson. I would have gone down with the original ship and most likely washed up on shore somewhere in lower Minnesota. You made it possible to finish my journey.

To Russ and the gang, The Monsters on Real Radio 104.1. My sincerest thanks for helping me share my story with more people than I could ever have reached on my own.

Thank you Ms. Wanda Hopkins for all your help with the original manuscript.

To the people of the river. I may not remember every name but the moments are written in my heart. Without your kindness and support, it would have been a lonely journey indeed... for what is a journey without human connection. Not one I wish to write.

I've saved this soul-deep thank you for last. Not because you were last on my mind but because your names deserve to linger in their hearts when this book is closed. Thank you Dr. Estelle Harris and team at the University of Utah Medical Center for saving my life. It's hard to write this sentence with dry eyes.

And a special thank you to Dr. Lee Zehngebot and Dr. James McClelland. You were there at the beginning and saw me through to the end.

Printed in the United States
By Bookmasters